Cyberschools:

An Education Renaissance

www.cyberschools.com

Also by Glenn R. Jones

Free Market Fusion

Make All America a School

*Jones Cable Television and Information
Infrastructure Dictionary*

*Jones Telecommunications and Multimedia
Encyclopedia (CD-ROM and Web Site)*

*Briefcase Poetry
Volumes 1-3*

Preface to the Second Edition

This 2nd edition of *Cyberschools: An Education Renaissance*, contains substantial updating of data in the figures and tables, plus new figures showing global Internet and computer growth and use. It also contains an expanded introduction and new technology descriptions, including a substantially rewritten Chapter 5 with a description of education delivery via the Web at JonesKnowledge.com. Analyses and discussions of the markets for distance learning in the U.S., Canada, China, Europe and Latin America also have been updated. A new Appendix B provides the credential criteria standards of the Global Alliance for Transnational Education. In the future, a portion of the time-sensitive information contained in this edition will be updated at the Web site www.cyberschools.com.

Cyberschools:
An Education Renaissance

www.cyberschools.com

Glenn R. Jones

With a Foreword by Alvin and Heidi Toffler

Second Edition
Cyber Publishing Group, Inc.
Englewood, Colorado

CYBER PUBLISHING GROUP, INC.
9697 E. MINERAL AVENUE, ENGLEWOOD, CO 80112

©1996, 1997, 1998, 2000 by Glenn R. Jones

Second paperback edition published in 2000, Cyber Publishing
Group, Inc.

Portions of *Cyberschools* appeared previously in *Make All America a
School,* published in 1991 by Jones 21st Century, Inc., a division of Jones
International™, Ltd., 9697 E. Mineral Avenue, Englewood, CO 80112.

ISBN: 1-885400-76-4

Library of Congress Catalog Card No.: 00-135131

Imagination is the most powerful human resource on the planet. Harnessing it and its resultant electronic tools in the service of education is the great hope of the world. This book is dedicated to the people who will make this hope a reality.

About the Author

Glenn R. Jones is founder and chief executive officer of JonesKnowledge.com™, and Jones International University™, whose subsidiaries and predecessors have been leaders in electronically delivered distance education since 1987. He was also the founder of Jones Intercable, Inc.

Mr. Jones has served on the board of directors and the executive committee of the National Cable Television Association, the boards of directors of Cable in the Classroom, and C-SPAN and on the boards of the National Alliance of Business and the American Society for Training and Development. He is founder of the Global Alliance for Transnational Education.

Mr. Jones has received awards for advancing minorities and women in media. He also has received several honorary doctoral degrees.

A graduate of the University of Colorado School of Law and the Stanford University Business School Executive Program, Mr. Jones is also the author of *Free Market Fusion, Make All America a School, Jones Cable Television and Information Infrastructure Dictionary, Jones Telecommunications and Multimedia Encyclopedia,* and several volumes of poetry.

CONTENTS

FOREWORD

Toward a Learning Community on the Planet

There are people who contribute greatly to society by thinking small — by focusing intensely on a set of narrow, sometimes incredibly complex, problems and working to solve them. There are others who contribute equally — and sometimes more — by thinking big. They tackle vast, recalcitrant, even more complex problems. Some, of course, do nothing but talk big dreams. Others work long and hard to make them come true and, for their trouble, are often dismissed as cranks, dreamers, or idealists. Some are. A few, however, are just the reverse.

Glenn Jones is one of these. A successful, hardheaded businessman, he built a large, important cable TV, telecommunications, and new media company starting from absolute scratch. That would be dream enough for most people. But Jones believes that the most successful businesses of the future — bigger and more profitable than today's giants — will be those that help solve crucial social crises — environmental issues, health issues, and, above all, the educational crisis.

Although almost everyone is dissatisfied with existing schools, colleges, and universities — not simply in the United States but across much of the world — most proposed innovations take for granted that educational problems can be solved within the existing framework.

Are our factory-style elementary and secondary schools in trouble? Increase homework. Increase teachers' pay. Patch up broken windows. In short, make the factory run faster.

Even as new technology and a Third Wave, knowledge-based economy move us from mass production of goods to customized or individualized production, children are still subjected to mass production education. (The idea of replacing the factory-style school with reconceptualized alternatives is still regarded as heresy by the educational establishment.)

Higher education, too, requires deep reconceptualization. Donald Langenberg, chancellor of the University of Maryland System and a former deputy director of the National Science Foundation, speculates that "many universities may die or may change beyond recognition as a result of the IT [information technology] revolution....Some may be 'virtual universities' that are delocalized across cyberspace." Which is what this book is about.

In public discourse, as in policy, "Education" with a capital E is regarded as a separate, specific category of social activity. "Media" are in another category. "Computers" are in still another category. Yet in the real world the boundaries among these categories are melting away. The world of computing and the world of media are converging. And it may be impossible to solve our most crucial social problems so long as we continue to think within the frame of these conventional categories.

Glenn Jones is a category-buster. And we believe, as he does, that education cannot be brought into the Third Wave future so long as it is viewed as separate from both the media and cyberspace.

In these pages, he lays out an exciting vision for the fusion of these activities into a worldwide education revolution. There is no single panacea for our problems. What Glenn Jones proposes cannot be expected to solve all the accumulated problems of our obsolete educational assembly lines. But it does offer high-powered tools to help people — not only the rich in the rich countries, but all people — gain access to better education at lower cost as a Third Wave learning community begins to form around the planet.

— Alvin and Heidi Toffler

ACKNOWLEDGMENTS

This book represents much of what I have learned about education, its complexity, and the transforming impact that technology is bringing to it.

In my global quest to find the keys to merging technology with education, I have met hundreds of fellow pilgrims. They included many leaders in business and academia, professor, teachers, UNESCO officers, high-technology practitioners, futurists, celebrities with educational perspectives, and innumerable politicians and regulators around the globe. Without listing them individually, I sincerely acknowledge their contributions, for they have demonstrated to me that there is good reason for hope in making all the world a school.

Specifically, I acknowledge my associates at the Jones companies and their commitment to JonesKnowledge.com™ and its affiliated companies and activities including Jones International University™– the University of the Web™; e-education™; e-global Library™; and Global Alliance of Transnational Education (GATE). They, through their imagination and endeavors, have orchestrated the concept of Cyberschools into marketable products. They are truly special, talented people, and I deeply appreciate their dedicated efforts.

Additionally, I would like to thank Jim Sample and Nancy Nachman-Hunt for their insights and their invaluable help in researching, refining, and helping to organize, develop, and polish the finished work; Nancy Zeilig and Sue Diehl for their professional and crucial copyediting; Barbara Scott for the typesetting, revisions, and editing suggestions on numerous proofs; the excellent research staffs of the World Bank and the United Nations Education, Scientific and Cultural Organization, which provided much of the data on education and population; and Kim Dority, who helped prepare an earlier book, *Make all America a School*, from which *Cyberschools* grew, and who provided early guidance and final review of the finished work.

Finally, I would like to acknowledge Ms. Dianne Eddolls, the lady in my life, for putting up with my intensity and the single-minded focus on *Cyberschools* that often consumed me.

There is only one good, knowledge, and one evil, ignorance.

> Socrates,
> in *Diogenes Laertius*

INTRODUCTION

Since Socrates first addressed the nature of knowledge, educators have struggled with two central questions: what to teach and how to teach it. The debate echoes from antiquity and volleys across today's mainstream bestsellers, exploding beyond the borders in town halls, corporate boardrooms, and even dining rooms throughout the world. The concept behind distance education offerings — frequently referred to as cyberschools in this book — is to deliver education to people instead of people to education.

This concept provides tested and proven answers to third and fourth questions: where should the learning take place and what constitutes learning?

In our global society, how these questions are answered has special significance because the answers will have a major impact on the many youthful, vibrant experiments with self-government, including the ongoing experiment with democracy in the United States. As historians Will and Ariel Durant pointed out more than two decades ago in *Lessons of History,* access to education is the key:

Table 1: World Education Demand and Media Penetration		
	1985	**1996**
Students/K–Higher	919 million	1.13 billion
Students/Higher	60.27 million	84.26 million
Television Sets (per 1,000 people)	154	236
Daily Newspapers (copies per 1,000 people)	95	96*

Source: UNESCO   *1994 data

> If equality of educational opportunity can be established, democracy will be real and justified. For this is the vital truth beneath its catchwords: that though men cannot be equal, their access to educational opportunity can be made more nearly equal.[1]

Our global cultures have undergone a transformation that lends great urgency to these questions. This transformation is our headlong race through an information revolution to a knowledge-based society (Table 1, Figures 1 and 2). This has created a sense that we are out of control. Decision-makers, who must in any event make decisions, are deluged with information they cannot grasp and with choices they do not comprehend. Everything is moving with great speed. There seems to be nothing to hold onto, and yet we must marvel at what is occurring.

TECHNOLOGY AS A TRANSFORMING FORCE

In a process that may be unique in the history of humankind, we have created technological capabilities that are transforming the globe. Land-line telephones in the early 1900s and television transmissions in the 1950s provided some rough context, but those technologies were quickly placed under the lock and key of traditional power interest. Perhaps the most important aspect of today's technologies is they proliferate beyond the control of traditional regulatory and industry cliques, though no small effort and expense are being expended to change that.

Most amazing, these changes have defied experts and pundits alike by progressing outside the bounds of any grand design, galvanized in many cases by the simple availability of fax machines, fiber-optic distribution systems, satellite TV dishes, computers, compact-disk players, and Internet connections. The change has come about at the grassroots level of the world's societies, implemented by people using these new tools to communicate about how and why to accomplish the things they care about.

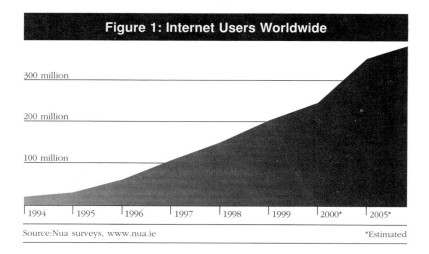

Figure 1: Internet Users Worldwide

300 million

200 million

100 million

1994 1995 1996 1997 1998 1999 2000* 2005*

Source:Nua surveys, www.nua.ie   *Estimated

DEMAND FOR HIGHER EDUCATION

Because of the rapid rise in literacy and education levels in many countries, North American, Western European, and Australian higher education has become a stable and lucrative export product. To illustrate, almost a half million of the United States' 14 million university enrollees are from other countries. Students are willing to travel great distances and in many cases commit themselves to years of government service in exchange for the financial support to enroll in traditional U.S., Canadian, European, and Australian degree programs on campus. We must think about how the opportunities for these students, and millions more who do not have the financial means for overseas study, will exponentially expand if they can begin to receive the same quality and content of coursework via electronic means, without the travel and at a fraction of the expense.

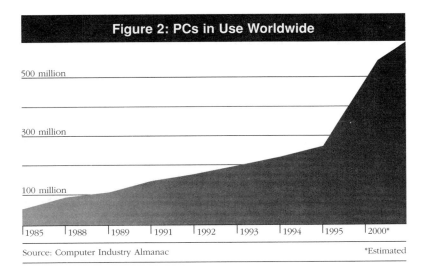

Figure 2: PCs in Use Worldwide

500 million

300 million

100 million

| 1985 | 1988 | 1989 | 1991 | 1992 | 1993 | 1994 | 1995 | 2000* |

Source: Computer Industry Almanac   *Estimated

For example, this electronic capability will make it possible for the great Asian universities to reach out to the rest of the world that needs to improve its understanding of Asian culture.

The demand for electronic delivery of all kinds of courses at all levels, including corporate training and K–12 classes, will mushroom now that we have entered the 21st century. Our global society's rate of technological adaptation is both driving that demand and providing the tools to present education via electronic media.

WHAT THE KNOWLEDGE SOCIETY DEMANDS

To understand this chicken-and-egg phenomenon, it is important to recognize some of the fundamental characteristics of our new knowledge society and the unique attributes that some Western-educated workers lend to this society.

The knowledge society we have entered differs greatly from the industrial society we leave behind. In the industrial society the principal resource was energy, and its tools were artifacts like forklifts, cranes, trucks, trains, automobiles, and airplanes. Its principal characteristic was that it allowed us to extend the human body.

The knowledge society is different because the velocity of its evolution is much more rapid, and its principal resource is information. Information is a special kind of resource. As has often been noted, it can be weightless, invisible, and in many different places at once. The tools of the information society drive the creation, storage, delivery, manipulation, and transformation of that information. Importantly, the principal characteristic of the knowledge revolution is that it allows us to dramatically extend the human mind by introducing a new model for learning.

The quantum extension of the human mind combined with the ability to extend the human body has resulted in a new reality, a reality in which the human mind, excluding religion and acts of nature, is now more clearly the most powerful force on the planet.

We are all integrally involved in this evolution, and education has an important part to play. Education is a process. Education is how information becomes meaningful. Information without meaning is useless. Education converts information into knowledge, understanding, and wisdom much like changing temperature turns water into ice. Education is the loom through which information is woven into value systems, dignity, self-worth, freedom, and into civilization itself.

THE KNOWLEDGE WORKER

Though all societies contribute to the evolution of education, economic and workforce experts claim that the developed world's universities produce graduates with unique capabilities.

The emergence of the "knowledge worker" college graduate, as first defined by Peter F. Drucker in his 1959 book, *Landmarks of Tomorrow,*[2] and later reexamined by Robert B. Reich in his 1991 book, *The Work of Nations: Preparing Ourselves for 21st Century Capitalism,* goes a long way toward describing the reasons why demand for the opportunity to receive college curriculum course content from the developed world's universities is so high.

The knowledge worker, or symbolic analyst as labeled by Reich, is that person who can produce new designs and concepts, as opposed to following standard procedures and producing familiar products.

Reich describes the demand for such an education:

> Millions of people across the globe are trying to learn symbolic-analytic skills, and many are succeeding. Researchers and engineers in East Asia and Western Europe are gathering valuable insights into microelectronics, macrobiotics, and new materials, and translating these insights into new products. Young people in many developing nations are swarming into universities to learn the symbolic and analytic secrets of design engineering, computer engineering, marketing, and management.[3]

With the continuing deployment of these sought-after educational experiences through distance learning and conventional class-room offerings, perhaps someday a society on a distant planet will seek to import the educational offerings that make possible our world's symbolic analyst learners.

A RENEWED FOCUS ON LEARNING

The evolution and continual specialization of our education processes in no way lessens the overall importance of education for the world as a whole. In fact, they intensify it.

Will and Ariel Durant stated it well:

If education is the transmission of civilization, we are unquestionably progressing. Civilization is not inherited; it has to be learned and earned by each generation anew; if transmission should be interrupted for one century, civilization would die, and we would be savages again. So our finest contemporary achievement is our unprecedented expenditure of wealth and toil in the provision of higher education for all.[4]

THE BRAIN UNDER SIEGE

The importance of general education is growing in tandem with the world's body of knowledge. Our libraries strain under the weight of books sounding the alarm about an information revolution and the speed at which new information is being generated.

By conservative estimate, the holdings of the world's libraries are doubling in volume every 14 years. At the end of the day, this information must be dealt with by an electrochemical contraption that weighs 3 pounds, more or less, takes up about half a cubic foot of space, runs on glucose at about 25 watts, processes information at the rate of approximately 100 quadrillion operations per second, looks like a big walnut, and is the world's first wet computer: the human brain. That brain is under siege, bombarded from all sides by torrents of new information.

The distance education approaches described in this book present an array of tools with which this vast body of knowledge can be considered, managed, and put to use by individuals. These tools can empower individuals by giving them the means to convert information into knowledge, understanding, and wisdom. They are technologies that can help spread out the decision-making process in governments, institutions, and businesses and can empower the individual.

Technological advances — especially the Internet and the myriad multimedia tools surrounding it, plus the many new enabling distribution systems — have created a communications environment in which vast amounts of information can be delivered inexpensively, an environment in which the barrier of distance is erased and the barrier of time is diminished. I refer to the various forms of fiber-optic and electronic information delivery as electronic platforms. The electronic platform is the new generation of the media delivery organization, and the phenomenon is rapidly finding adaptations in the education sector.

DEFINING EDUCATION

The convergence of technology and education has precipitated an active assault on the traditional concept of learning. Certainly the "out of control" school of alarmists has reason to be concerned. Although technology provides wonderful opportunities for communication, research, and multimedia displays, it is also available to those who can — and do — abuse it under the name of "education."

Diploma mills have proliferated for more than 300 years and now can dispense ad hoc degrees-on-a-disk or doctorates by e-mail. And, racing to shelter under the education umbrella, even TV executives claim that much of what they do is in the name of learning and furthering viewers' cultural horizons. Is all information education? Possibly. Should all information be accorded similar levels of respect and credence by education and media organizations? Unequivocally, no.

Just as college credits are sometimes inappropriately given to students for completely irrelevant "life experience," a broadcast of "The Sword of Zorro" as an education program represents an abuse.

At the same time, education and consumer groups alike should expect and demand reasonable and expedient open certification of distance education offerings. To pretend that certification does not matter, that it will be granted in due time, is to invite failure in our response to the needs of the world's rapidly growing class of 21st century lifelong learners.

We are blazing through an information revolution that is technology-driven. If we don't measure up to the responsibilities of leadership in the content we select and develop to distribute through our new technology, the knowledge society will fall far below its potential.

Revolutions are transitory. Though this may come as a surprise to many media and technology zealots, the information revolution is already waning. Technologies will continue to be invented and to proliferate, but the fundamental restructuring of the world's economic and political systems already has been set in motion. The result is rapidly unfolding around us, a knowledge-based society that is the legacy ascendant of the revolution.

THE CRITICAL ISSUE: SPEED

Critical issues must be addressed to ensure the quality of our educational processes and content. Fortunately, our current focus has come to be exploring how quickly and effectively education can be delivered.

This issue was stated in economic terms by William B. Johnston and Arnold H. Packer in their landmark study *Workforce 2000,* which cited education and training as the primary systems by which human capital is both developed and protected.[5] The speed and efficiency with which these systems transmit knowledge and influence the rate of growth in human capital are more important than the traditional gauge of rate of investment in plant and equipment, the same study noted.

It is the obligation and opportunity of every person and organization committed to the concept of self-government and to the forward progress of civilization to lend what tools they can to assist in the education of humankind. The challenges are what, how, where, and when to teach for optimum benefit. The solutions will benefit individual learners, the institution of self-government, and civilization.

ASKING QUESTIONS BEYOND THE WEB

While we grappled with student demographics for the coming decade and evaluated software vendors and potential partners, the idea of the university on the Web has rapidly changed from concept to reality. Such a university is much more than Web pages and streams of e-mail, though these tools are opening doors at a breakneck pace, and their technological successors will surely accelerate the change.

The university on the Web is a dynamic learning environment that requires the full engagement of the faculty and students who use it. It must be supported by a technical and administrative cadre who interact with faculty and students constantly in order to ensure that a quality education is the final outcome.

I foresee a day when the universities on the Web and traditional on-campus education will blend together seamlessly as a result of technology enhancements and of institutions and businesses joining together in the pursuit of academic excellence. As a step in this direction, I would like to suggest three questions for students and educators to ask themselves and their colleagues as they pursue electronic education approaches and evolve their own technological capabilities at the dawn of the new millennium:

Who "owns" the knowledge that resides in our institutions of higher learning — the institution, the faculty, or the students to whom it is imparted?

Can we learn to embrace change while continuing to respect our traditions?

Are we prepared to deal with shifts in societal demands and new technology that will dwarf the changes we witnessed to date?

The Lesson of Athens

Imagine the vibrant energy and intellect of Athens during the time of Socrates and Plato. The ghost of Athens is visible today.

It has been said that Plato, in all his strivings to imagine an ideal training school, failed to notice that Athens itself was a greater school than even he could dream of.

Let us notice *our* environment. It is time now to fuse our knowledge society's electronic tools with our great teaching institutions and information repositories. It is time to create a world that is, like Athens was, a great school, a world vibrant with interest and excitement about education, a world where educational opportunity is visible to all and hope is alive, a world that sees the wilderness of information as its new frontier.

---

[1]Will and Ariel Durant, *The Lessons of History* (New York: Simon and Schuster, 1968), 79.

[2]Peter F. Drucker, *Landmarks of Tomorrow* (New York: Harper & Row, 1959).

[3]Robert B. Reich, *The Work of Nations: Preparing Ourselves for 21st Century Capitalism* (New York: Alfred A. Knopf, 1991), 225.

[4]W. and A. Durant, *Lessons of History,* 101.

[6]William B. Johnston and Arnold H. Packer, *Workforce 2000: Work and Workers for the Twenty-first Century* (Indianapolis, Ind.: Hudson Institute, 1987), xxvii.

**There is no domestic knowledge
and no international knowledge.
There is only knowledge.**

> — Peter F. Drucker,
> in *The Atlantic Monthly*

THE GLOBAL EDUCATION CHALLENGE

The dawning of any century can be counted on to elicit prophecies and prognostications from all manner of philosophers, poets, and pontificators. For the world of higher education, the predictions are that schools and universities worldwide are going to be faced with educating more people with fewer dollars for longer periods of time and then finding them back again a few years later for more.

History provides the evidence that these forecasts are right. In essence, higher education in the 21st century is finding itself playing a game of catch-up. The destruction and death wrought by World War II in Europe, Asia, and Africa left those continents and their societies years behind in their development of key competencies, including educational infrastructure and programs. Beginning in the late 1960s — reflecting the 20-plus years it took for many countries just to produce new college-age generations — the world's educational institutions began to respond to new demands.

The following three decades saw the demand for education evolve at an alarming rate. Between 1985 and 1996 alone, the

1

Table 2: World Education — Vital Statistics			
	1985	**1996**	**% increase**
Population	4.9 billion	5.7 billion	14
Students/K-Higher*	919 million	1.13 billion	14
Students/Higher*	60.27 million	84.26 million	28
Percent of World's GNP Used for Education	4.9%	5.1%*	0.2
Source: UNESCO			*1992 data

world's total student body, preschool through all types of higher education, grew by 209 million, from 919 million to 1.13 billion (Table 2). That was a 14 percent increase in just 11 years.[1]

There also has been a tremendous and encouraging increase in the enrollments of primary and secondary students, particularly in developing countries, and the world's literacy level is improving steadily (Table 3). Most astounding is that the number of students seeking higher education — including vocational training and university certificate and degree programs — grew 28 percent during the same 11-year period, adding 24 million students (Table 2). That's the highest growth rate of any single educational sector.

Driven by world population growth, improving literacy rates, and desires for growth in personal incomes, the demand for higher education continues to grow (Table 4). During the 1985–96 period, the number of students enrolled in secondary education grew 24 percent, from 291 million to 381.9 million,[2] and some educational analysts anticipate that at least 30 percent of these second-

2

ary-level students will want some form of higher education in the early 21st century.

THE NEW ADULT LEARNER

But secondary school graduates are by no means the only segment of the world's population seeking higher education. Let's look at how the world's student body has changed over the past generation.

Table 3: World Literacy			
	1980	**2000 (projected)**	**% increase**
World	69.6%	79.4%	9.8
Developed Countries	96.6%	98.9%	2.3
Developing Countries	58%	73.4%	15.4
China	66%	85%	19
India	40.8%	55.8%	15

Source: *World Education Report*, 1995

Our past assumptions about who the typical college student was and how, when, why, and where that student attended college are no longer valid. Today the world's colleges and universities are faced with new student body demographics. This trend coincides with the arrival of the digital age.

There are at least three typical global higher education student profiles. One is Asian as its dominant trait; another is over 23 years

3

of age; and the third holds an associate-equivalent or bachelor's degree and either has been or is about to be "downsized" from a job.

These student profiles share two common traits: Their current educational pursuits include a heavy component of technology-related courses — engineering, health care, or computer — and they are paying a significant portion of their tuition out of their own pockets via personal savings, loans, or assistance from their families.

In addition, as the average college student age of 23 indicates, we no longer define a college education as something we do between the ages of 18 and 22. We have come to understand and embrace the concept of "lifelong learning."[3] Indeed, lifelong learning has moved from the category of "discretionary" personal investment to "essential" as people scramble to bolster their credentials in a volatile global workplace.

Upward mobility through education is not just a tactic of white-collar management and computer professionals, either. Professionals looking for educational options range from nurse practitioners

Table 4: World Higher Education — Student Growth			
	1985	**1996**	**% increase**
Africa	2.19 million	4.33 million	51
Asia	20.04 million	32.58 million	38
Europe/Russia Fed.	17.3 million	21.34 million	19
Latin America	6.36 million	8.78 million	28
North America	20.25 million	24.81 million	18
World	60.27 million	84.26 million	28

Source: UNESCO

to golf course groundskeepers and from sanitation and environmental technicians to assistant chefs.

For a number of reasons (one being an aging Western population and another being the view outside the industrialized world that college education is an import, versus export, industry), many countries now are turning their attention to providing education that will keep their college students and their educational dollars at home, rather than shipping them out to Los Angeles or Paris.

Another interesting dimension to the growing demand for education is that although the developing world's student population is young, the priorities placed on education and continued improvement by all societies suggest that this large and rapidly growing young student body represents a long-term market for lifelong learning programs.

Some educational authorities describe the "bubble" of Western baby boomers who are demanding lifelong learning options as though it is a phenomenon that might disappear into retirement homes in the next 30 years. This is a mistake.

In some academic circles, there resides the faulty assumption that, within a generation or so, the world's student bodies will have returned to traditional colleges because their campuses are the only bona fide educational source. This assumption fails to take into account both the characteristics of the rest of the world's lifelong learners and the societal and economic forces that will drive them over the next 20 years. At the very least, lifelong learners among the Western baby boomers will soon be joined and eventually eclipsed by seekers of education from developing countries in both East and West Asia and, eventually, Africa.

To meet both the short-term and long-term demand, countries must either build universities and staff them with world-class faculty or augment their higher educational institutions with less expensive alternatives. Distance education — the delivery of educational courses from one location to students at another location — is an alternative. Within distance education, cyberschools are a relatively new concept because they offer educational content and classes that are conducted electronically, and they are definitely an economical option.

PUBLIC FINANCING

Cyberschools have appeared at an opportune moment in history. Statistics show that public financing for education the world over is shrinking. In the late 1980s and early 1990s public financing to support the global educational system grew in total outlay, but at a much slower rate than demand. Despite the rapid influx of students, governments and taxpayers worldwide increased support to education by only 0.2 percent of their gross national products (GNPs).

Part of that low rate of increase can be attributed to demand outstripping supply, but even more of it can be assigned to antiquated models for building educational infrastructure. Some education leaders insisted that education at all levels — and accredited courses in particular — be delivered only by providing traditional bricks-and-mortar campuses with class ratios and class environments approved by faculty committees and administrators. These educational Luddites completely missed the boat in understanding the type of global societal change driving educational demand and what must be done to respond to it.

The quality of educational content and delivery has been and should always be the first concern. Likewise, there always will be a place for traditional campuses and classroom settings. But 21st century students need varied classroom environments and diverse educational delivery systems. There is no one way courses must be taught, so long as students learn and can demonstrate their learning through accredited testing and examination procedures.

Globally, fiscal concerns will increasingly drive the delivery of education. Shrinking fiscal support for education in developed and

Table 5: 1995 Global GNP Growth and Higher Education Students				
Country	GNP Growth	Population in millions	Students in millions	% in Higher Education
China	11.8%	1,210	2.5	0.2%
India	5.0%	952	21.3	2.2%
Indonesia	6.7%	207	1.9	0.1%
Japan	0.6%	125	4.2	3.4%
Korea	7.6%	45	1.8	4.0%
Malaysia	8.4%	20	0.2	1.0%
Philippines	4.3%	75	1.9	2.5%
Thailand	8.6%	59	0.7	1.2%
United States	3.3%	300	14.0	4.7%

Source: World Bank, Pacific Economic Cooperation Council, and analysts' estimates

developing countries alike makes it crucial that new models for education incorporate delivery by both traditional institutions and carefully integrated electronic platforms. (The term electronic platform, as it applies to education, refers to the technology that makes possible electronic delivery using any, or any combination of, a wide array of telecommunications systems, including, without limitations, broadcast, satellite, cable television, radio, telephone, computer, and the Internet.)

A comparison of GNP growth with 1995 percentages of population enrolled in higher education throughout the world suggests an imminent explosion in demand (Table 5). Although the level of public financing for higher education has plateaued in many countries and in some countries has even decreased concurrently with unprecedented demand for education, alarmed pundits ignore three crucial facts:

- First, students of enormously varying financial means are finding ways to attain higher levels of education, often without the public financing support of a decade ago.

- Second, in this era of public budget deficits, public financing for education — in most countries — is constrained and certainly is not likely to increase at the same rate as the demand for education, no matter how shrill the alarms. The private sector, from small private universities and polytechnics to electronic colleges offering on-line courses and degrees, is already offering alternatives.

- Third, in many cases, especially with developing countries, public funds are being redirected to pre-primary, primary, and secondary education and away from higher education in an effort to improve basic literacy and student income-producing capability. This change in priorities is supported by both World Bank and UNESCO educational study recommendations.[4]

There is good reason to argue that public funding cannot, and need not, keep pace, even at the secondary level. The United States in particular probably spent too many dollars on education during the 1970s and 1980s, with dubious benefits in some cases.

A special report on world education published by *The Economist* magazine in 1992 noted that although the United States had the highest level of per-pupil public dollars — about $6,000 per student — for primary and secondary students of all the industrialized nations, it also had the highest level of high school dropouts at 14 percent and a notoriously underqualified fledgling workforce. U.S. university students and graduates ranked somewhat better, albeit with less dependence on public funding. Japan and Germany both spent far less in public funds educating their students with better results in terms of workforce skills, the report noted.[5]

Throwing public funds at the U.S. educational problem, *The Economist* editors concluded, does not seem to be a prescription for success. At the higher education level, high costs also are contentious and have reached the point of limiting access. One partial solution to the financial access barrier is to adopt additional ways to augment higher education venues, ways that include the use of technology available through private-sector educational alternatives.

LESSONS FROM THE WORLD BANK

In 1994, the International Bank for Reconstruction and Development (IBRD), part of the World Bank, released *Higher Education: The Lessons of Experience,* a report that spelled out the bank's successes and failures in helping underwrite higher education in developing countries. Noting that direct investments in traditional higher education had sometimes produced disappointing or hard-to-define results, the report lauded distance learning approaches in developing countries:

> Distance education and open learning programs can be effective in increasing access, at modest cost, for underprivileged groups that are usually poorly represented in university enrollments... distance education can be an effective way also to provide lifelong education and upgrade skills, as when used for in-service teacher training. [Since 1970] distance education has rapidly expanded in Bangladesh, China, India, Indonesia, Korea, Pakistan, the Philippines, Sri Lanka, and Thailand. [Thailand's two open universities] have been the government's principal instrument for expanding access to students from the poorest social strata, especially in urban areas. Operating on a self-financing basis, the open universities account for 62 percent of Thailand's higher education enrollments. Distance education programs can also be designed with a regional (multinational) clientele. For example, UNISA, the Open University of South Africa, draws 15,000 of its 120,000 students from neighboring countries.[6]

Such programs, the report noted, are usually much less expensive than conventional university programs because of much higher student–teacher ratios. The report stated there was an international higher education crisis: shrinking funds to meet a growing demand. It discussed various causes and effects, but pinpointed two key facets of the crisis:

- Developing countries that had funded higher education to the detriment of primary and secondary education were not experiencing comparable increases in jobs requiring college degrees; and

- Funds for higher education in most countries were decreasing, especially government-funded degree and grant programs, placing more students in the status of self-reliant.[7]

Although deploring the decline in funding for public education in most countries, the IBRD report noted that private institutions have been a key remedy in some countries, at little or no direct public cost.[8] This is part of the evidence that, once above literacy and secondary-education levels, students will do their best to pay for their own education and vocational and professional continuing study programs, providing these programs can be delivered at a reasonable cost. These are important points, too often played down when remedies to the crisis in public education are sought, especially if public funding is involved.

Additionally, when institutions rely heavily on government funding, their programs can sometimes reflect a to-be-expected but unfortunate bias that does not necessarily reflect the interests of students. Two years prior to IBRD's report on higher education, *The Economist* magazine's 1992 report had noted that educational reformers in developed countries were having a hard time coming up with solutions that budgets could solve, regardless of the availability of public funds.[9]

In any case, it is unlikely that financing from the public sector is going to experience a significant change. The better we understand the nature of the market demand for education and the more we recognize that increased funding is no sure-fire remedy for education at any level, the better our chances of applying cost-effective remedies that reflect present realities.

OLDER STUDENTS: BUDGET-MINDED LEARNERS

For at least some of the U.S. higher education establishment, economic reality is about to arrive in the form of a degreed student who must retrain to keep a job and doesn't have time or money for campus frills.

When the first edition of this book was prepared in mid-1996, researchers found more than one source that predicted enrollment of the "traditional" student in colleges and universities would dwindle. As late as 1979 in the United States, traditional full-time students, 18 to 22 years old and usually straight out of high school, numbered 4.5 million. One source predicted that by 1992, enrollment of traditional students would fall from the 1979 high down to 3.1 million, a decline of 32 percent.[10]

Statistics available in mid-2000, when the current edition was prepared, showed that not only did the decline not occur but there has been a considerable increase in demand for education for both full-time and part-time students. According to the *Chronicle of Higher Education*, full-time enrollment in two- and four-year institutions for traditional full-time students, 18 to 22 years old, grew to almost 5.8 million in 1998, with another 700,000 students in the same age category attending part-time. Older age groups saw an even more dramatic change, with the National Center for Education Statistics reporting that, in 1998, 45 percent of all post-secondary students were working adults 25 years of age or older.

The most encouraging news is that more adults than ever before are seeking an education, motivated by an increasingly technology-driven employment marketplace that has less and less room for those who try to compete with just high school–level skills. Also, the demand for part-time college-level education has grown right along.

Traditional full-time students in the 18 to 22 age category represent a relatively static demographic group — less than 2 percent growth annually is projected between 1998 and 2006, a function of lower birthrates among baby boomers. However, the baby boomers themselves and "graying" Generation Xers in the form of adult learners are stepping in to fill the void. These students are typically 25 to 35 years old and are employed at least part time. Many of them have employers who are paying some or all of their educational costs. These students deal with scheduling conflicts, difficulties in getting to campus, geographical relocation brought on by job transfers, and frequently the extra demands of parenthood. By 2006, there will be an increased demand for 1.1 million classroom spaces in the United States for college education of all types. Much of this increased demand will be met by distance learning courses (Figure 3). In 2002, there will be 2.2 million college distance education enrollments, up from 710,000 in 1998.

Adult learners typically have little interest in the expensive "extras" of college such as social and athletic events, association with sororities or fraternities, and various other on-campus organizations and activities. They need flexible scheduling, affordable prices, and attendance options. In many cases, the existence of college libraries and bookstores are conveniences they will gladly forgo, providing they can receive reference materials and study assignments by postal service or, increasingly, over the Internet. Such students exist in all types and levels of education, and they are found virtually all around the globe.

Ken Dychtwald and Joe Flower in their book *Age Wave* described this changing approach to education:

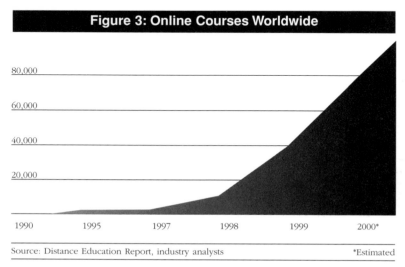

Figure 3: Online Courses Worldwide

80,000					
60,000					
40,000					
20,000					
1990	1995	1997	1998	1999	2000*

Source: Distance Education Report, industry analysts · *Estimated

You may stop working one or more times in your thirties, forties, or fifties in order to go back to school, raise a second (or third) family, enter a new business, or simply to take a couple of years to travel and enjoy yourself. You may go back to work in your sixties, seventies, or even eighties. You may find that the traditional framework of life — with youth the time for learning, adulthood for nonstop working and raising a family, and old age for retirement — will come unglued, offering new options at every stage. A cyclic life arrangement will replace the current linear life plan as people change direction and take up new challenges many times in their lives.[11]

In fact, numerous studies undertaken in the past several years by industry groups, governments, public institutions, and private foundations are projecting that by the year 2020 the average worker will undergo *at least* five major job changes in his or her lifetime.

WHAT HIGHER EDUCATION TARGETS

Traditionally, most North American universities target graduating high school students as their prime market for recruiting. With lower birthrates since 1970, that pool of higher education prospects has stabilized. At the same time, another dynamic has been at work. Those who earned their degrees or began earning them in the 1960s, '70s and '80s are now changing careers, seeking more training and education to sustain and excel in their chosen fields, and making plans to work beyond the once mandatory retirement age of 65. To do this, they are looking for accessible degree completion programs and new career education opportunities.

And North American employers are contributing to this trend by extending retirement ages in order to fill critical labor force shortages and keep on tap a highly experienced pool of talent. They are also increasing their corporate training budgets. There are now more than 1,600 corporate training universities or academies, up from just 400 in 1988. They spend about $200 billion annually on their training programs, which is about one-third of all funds spent on postsecondary education.[12]

The advertising industry is beginning to respond to the graying of the world's population as well. The target age span demographic for many Madison Avenue agency brand campaigns has now been broadened from the 18 to 49 range all the way to 54. If Mick Jagger, a 54-year-old grandfather, can still pack a stadium, who can afford to ignore the trend?

In the United States, college enrollment for students 65 and older jumped 27 percent from 1991 to 1995. The U.S. Department of Education says some 81,000 people over 65 are now part-time or full-time college students, and another 356,000 students are age 50 to 64.[13]

THE GRAYING DEMOGRAPHIC TREND

We know that the graying demographic trend is not limited to North America and Europe. East Asia's current population of 2 billion is largely the result of increasingly low mortality rates since the end of World War II, in spite of some more recent cataclysmic events such as the Vietnam War and Cambodia's Khmer Rouge purges that took a heavy toll.

According to Nicholas Eberstadt, writing in the periodical *The National Interest*,[14] East Asia's demographic profile between 1998 and 2015 will shift upward to a median age of 37.[15] This is several years older than the current American median and similar to the present demographic of Eastern Europe. At the same time, falling or stabilizing birthrates in East Asia mean there will be fewer young students graduating from institutions to nudge their elders into retirement and help support them once they do retire.

One of the solutions will be to continue to educate and retrain older adults to keep them in the Asian workplace. This would require a conventional educational infrastructure several times the size of what the region now supports in order to keep older adult productivity at a desirable level. Electronically delivered education via the Internet, computers, televisions, and videocassette recorders can help supply some of this infrastructure quickly and at a comparatively low cost as an alternative to bricks-and-mortar classroom buildings. Although West Asia, Africa, and Central Asia currently have different population dynamics, they can be expected to eventually follow similar trends as they find the right formulas to match educational investments with human capital needs and follow the path to prosperity.

In North America, one interesting trend has remained consistent as the student age demographic has changed. Older adult students still want the same things they did when the postal service was the only means of distance education delivery: education access at an affordable cost.

Germany and Japan present the most obvious examples of varying attitudes toward education — varying compared with the norms of the United States and the United Kingdom — that have been successful in terms of standards of living and GNP. Both countries surpass the U.S. and British standards of living, yet each has different approaches to education and workforce training. Based on that country's long tradition of apprenticeship, in Germany workers expect and receive considerable ongoing training throughout their careers, most paid for by the government and their employers.

In Japan, the country's rigorous secondary school system produces graduates with what some estimate is the equivalent of a U.S. four-year college education. This explains why large Japanese companies expect new employees, just out of high school, to be capable of immediately completing an engineering course of study before assuming their places on the factory floors.[16]

Other European and Asian countries have developed similar systems, and most are now integrating continuing education into their workforce training programs. As industrialized nations transform into knowledge-based economies and developing countries undertake mainline manufacturing, higher education institutions worldwide must make comparable shifts in the way they deliver their educational products. It is a difficult transition that must simultaneously address technology adaptation and confront deeply entrenched perceptions on more traditional campuses.

[1]UNESCO, UNESCO Statistical Yearbook 1998, http://unescostat.unesco.org/yearbook/ybindexnew.htm

[2]Ibid.

[3]For detailed discussions of the importance of lifelong learning to the U.S. economy, see James Botkin et al., *Global Stakes: The Future of High Technology in America* (Cambridge, Mass.: Ballinger Publishing Company, 1982); William B. Johnston and Arnold H. Packer, *Workforce 2000: Work and Workers for the Twenty-first Century* (Indianapolis, Ind.: Hudson Institute, 1987), xxvi–xxvii and 95–103; Jack E. Bowsher, *Educating America: Lessons Learned in the Nation's Corporations* (New York: John Wiley & Sons, Inc., 1989), 208–220; and *A Nation at Risk: The Full Account* (Cambridge, Mass.: USA Research, for The National Commission on Excellence in Education, 1984).

[4]International Bank for Reconstruction and Development, *Higher Education: The Lessons of Experience* (Washington, D.C., 1994).

[5]A Survey of Education," *The Economist*, 28 November 1992.

[6]International Bank, *Higher Education*, 33.

[7]Ibid., 16–19.

[8]Ibid., 34.

[9]Survey of Education," *Economist*, 7.

[10]For an analysis of the changing ratio of older students to traditional students and of the effects of the change, see Arthur Levine and Associates, *Shaping Higher Education's Future: Demographic Realities and Opportunities, 1990–2000* (San Francisco, Jossey-Bass Publishers, 1989), and current issues of *The Chronicle of Higher Education* (weekly, 1255 23rd St., Washington, D.C. 20037).

[11]Ken Dychtwald and Joe Flower, *Age Wave: The Challenges and Opportunities of an Aging America* (Los Angeles: Jeremy P. Tarcher, Inc., 1989), 3.

[12]"Corporate Universities Multiplying Rapidly," Reuters, August 18, 1998.

[13]"Late-Blooming Scholars," *Business Week*, July 20, 1998, p. 106.

[14]Nicholas Eberstadt, "Asia tomorrow, gray and male. (demographic trends in East Asia)," *The National Interest*, fall 1998, p. 56.

[15]Ibid.

[16]Ray Marshall and Marc Tucker, *Thinking for a Living: Education and the Wealth of Nations* (New York: Basic Books, a division of HarperCollins Publishers, Inc., 1992), 44, 49.

The price tag for a four-year undergraduate degree can now run as high as $100,000.

> — William E. Simon,
> Former Secretary of the
> U.S. Treasury and President,
> John M. Olin Foundation,
> in *The Wall Street Journal*

2

The Costs/Benefits Equation

It is not an overstatement to say that a college education is becoming what it was 100 years ago: prohibitively expensive to all but the world's most well off.

U.S. Higher Education Meets the Bottom Line

Higher education in the United States alone is an increasingly troubled $213 billion industry.[1] Other countries' higher education systems also face severe budget constraints. I offer this focused look at the U.S. education dilemma because it is a bellwether for the world's other education markets and, if solutions emerge, can offer a paradigm for change.

Perhaps the most pressing concern regarding higher education is the astounding increase in the costs of attending college. The 1980s saw health-care costs rise a whopping 117 percent, but the price of an education at a private college jumped 146 percent, and the average cost of attending a public college increased by 109 percent.[2]

Today, annual tuition and fees at public four-year institutions equal 9 percent of the median American family income; attending a private institution requires 38 percent of the median family income.[3] College costs continue to outdistance inflation, and their rapid increase effectively denies educational opportunity to those unable to afford the escalating expense.

These statistics represent a national crisis: Education is one of the few industries in the United States that has become less rather than more productive. This is not a minor issue, because higher education employs some 2 million people, a third of them faculty members, and annually enrolls nearly 14 million students. Thus about 5 percent of the U.S. population either works or studies within the higher education structure.

Part of the problem with costs relates to the expansion and upgrading undertaken by U.S. colleges and universities in the past two decades. These were necessary in order to meet the growing enrollment of baby boom students and to remain academically competitive.

In its quest for quality the higher education system has invested in advanced technology and costly physical plants that often sit unused for four or five months each year. This problem will worsen as empty residence halls, no longer filled with traditional college-age students, continue to incur maintenance costs.

At the same time access to higher education for geographically distant students, those who must travel, and others who cannot attend campus-held classes has become a high priority. As Americans recognize the importance of a college education to their careers, to their quality of life, to their economy, and to their children's futures, they are increasingly concerned about universal access to higher education. In an increasingly competitive world economy, the United States cannot let people with potential drop out of the educational system. If, indeed, they do, they also drop out of the economic system at ever-more unpalatable costs to society. This point was dramatically made by Johnston and Packer in *Workforce 2000* in their prediction that:

> During the 1985–2000 period, the good fortune to be born in or to immigrate to the United States will make less difference than the luck or initiative to be well-educated and well-trained. For individuals, the good jobs of the future will belong to those who have skills that enable them to be productive in a high-skill, service economy. For the nation, the success with which the workforce is prepared for high-skilled jobs will be an essential ingredient in maintaining a high-productivity, high-wage economy.[4]

UNIVERSITY TEACHER SHORTAGES

Another change affecting higher education is the teacher shortage predicted to last at least through 2010. In *Prospects for Faculty in the Arts and Sciences*,[5] co-authors William Bowen and Julie Ann Sosa confirmed what educators had suspected for several years: By the late 1990s, a substantially increasing rate of enrollment in higher education resulted in major shortages of faculty members at colleges throughout the United States. Similar shortages are expected in other countries, where college enrollments already strain the capacities of campuses to deliver in-person instruction.

As the children of the 77 million baby boomers move through U.S. colleges and universities, they will expand demand for faculty at the same time that many professors, hired to meet the baby boom demand of the 1960s and 1970s, are scheduled to retire. Unless a means is found to deliver education to more students without radically increasing the number of faculty, many would-be students will be closed out of the higher education system.

WORKER RETRAINING: AN INTERNATIONAL MARKET

Business and labor leaders recognize the importance of retraining workers with skills that meet 21st century employment needs.[6] The educational imperative for workers applies to both industrialized and developing countries and their workers. According to *Workers in an Integrating World*, a 1995 report by the

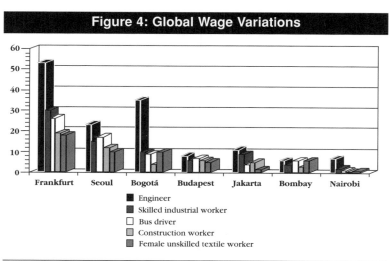

Figure 4: Global Wage Variations

Engineer
Skilled industrial worker
Bus driver
Construction worker
Female unskilled textile worker

Note: Earnings in selected occupations in seven cities have been adjusted to reflect purchasing power parity. Data are for 1994.
Source: Union Bank of Switzerland, 1994

24

World Bank, in virtually every country, more highly educated workers *who are employed* make the most money (Figure 4).[7] However, the World Bank also found that in some developing countries such as India, Bangladesh, and Mexico, there are many over-educated workers and too few job opportunities because high illiteracy rates elsewhere in their societies are a drag on their economies.

There is now a consensus that nearly 50 percent of U.S. workers are employed in some aspect of the "knowledge," or "information," economy, although the definition of what constitutes "information work" is undergoing continued re-evaluation.[8] Consequently, the United States' competitive edge in what is now a global marketplace is based on its ability to teach workers not just to be technically proficient, but to think, to evaluate, to adapt, to use information resources, and to become lifelong learners. A similar transformation is under way in the European Union countries, Canada, Japan, and Singapore.

These skills are critical in all areas of industry, not just among top-level management.

Economists estimate that as many as 40 million people were dislocated by the "restructuring" in world manufacturing from 1980 to 1995. In *Thriving on Chaos*, Tom Peters noted that "since 1980, the Fortune 500 have shed a staggering 2.8 million jobs."[9] Peters's book was published in 1987. In the 1990s, another 3.1 million people were laid off by corporate America, according to the Chicago-based outplacement firm Challenger, Gray, and Christmas. More restructuring will take place as these companies respond to marketplace demand and further competitive threats.

The changing nature and skill requirements of the U.S. workplace were comprehensively documented by Johnston and Packer in *Workforce 2000:*

> As the economies of developed nations move further into the post-industrial era, human capital plays an ever-more-important role in their progress. As the society becomes more complex, the amount of education and knowledge needed to make a productive contribution to the economy becomes greater.[10]

Later in their analysis, Johnston and Packer stated:

> The jobs that will be created between 1987 and 2000 will be substantially different from those in existence today. A number of jobs in the least-skilled job classes will disappear, while high-skilled professions will grow rapidly. Overall, the skill mix of the economy will be moving rapidly upscale, with most new jobs demanding more education and higher levels of language, math and reasoning skills. Among the fastest-growing jobs, the trend toward higher educational requirements is striking. Of all the new jobs that will be created over the 1983–2000 period, more than half will require some education beyond high school, and almost a third will be filled by college graduates. Today, only 22 percent of all occupations require a college degree.[11]

The changes forecast by Johnston and Packer are occurring throughout the developed, industrialized world among workers seeking better skills and employers wanting more productivity. As countries struggle to define their positions as both trading partners and international competitors, they also are challenged to transform their educational systems to respond to a global economy with shifting and disappearing boundaries.

Clearly, new tools and concepts are required to master this rampant change in our environment. Higher levels of education are imperative for workers in every upward-developing country.

The turbulence of change and the need to adjust are manifest. Yet, for the worker who needs retraining, the military man or woman, the rural adult learner, shift workers, homebound parents, the gifted high school student with no opportunity to take college-level classes at his or her high school, and various others, access to educational opportunities generally and to college coursework and credit specifically has been difficult, if not impossible.

Indeed, as I have noted, at the end of the 20th century, higher education was close to becoming the privilege it was at the century's beginning. This does not need to be the case, however. Higher education for the smallest number would be a tragic legacy for us to leave succeeding generations required to compete in the global economy of the 21st century.

ELEMENTARY AND SECONDARY EDUCATION

Elementary and secondary schools in the United States have also had to grapple with shifting circumstances. U.S. schools have attempted to meet two important goals: enriching the classroom experience and providing access to education to a wide and varied population. In addition, these two issues, frequently referred to as "excellence and equity," have been accompanied by a host of other considerations.

State-mandated changes. New, state-mandated changes in curriculum call for more breadth and depth in courses that schools, particularly at the secondary level, are required to offer. These reforms affect schools of every town, city, county, and school district in America.

Requirements for high school graduation have been radically upgraded in many states, with special emphasis placed on mathematics, science, and languages. State colleges and universities across the country also are emphasizing the importance of these subjects by elevating admission requirements in these areas. Unfortunately, the task of meeting requirements at both the secondary and college levels is aggravated by a shortage of appropriate teachers and by budgetary pressures.

In addition to the curricular changes called for, most states now require teachers to participate in professional development or in-service training courses on a regular basis. The importance of professional development cannot be underestimated: To keep pace with the expanding educational requirements of their students, teachers must stay current with the most recent advances in their fields. Yet, for many teachers such courses are unavailable, inaccessible, or at best inconvenient.

Teacher shortages and budget constraints. As noted in *Linking for Learning*, the report on distance education issued in 1989 by the U.S. Department of Commerce's Office of Technology Assessment,

Shifting economic and demographic patterns have left many small and rural schools with declining student populations and even more limited financial and instructional resources. Solutions such as school consolidation or transporting students or teachers have often been stretched to their geographic limits; these approaches are also disruptive and politically unpopular.[12]

Yet these schools must provide the basics of a good education and, if possible, broaden their students' intellectual exposure beyond the confines of their immediate locales.

Struggling to provide a basic education to all students, many schools have few remaining resources with which to meet the unique needs of individuals who either have difficulty learning or are intellectually gifted. This is especially true for schools located in areas that are culturally isolated, economically disadvantaged, or both.

When resources must be stretched just to address the needs of the majority of students, gifted students, some of whom perhaps have the potential to provide signature insights about our world and its problems, may go unchallenged. This is a painful situation because, unless such students are challenged early, their ability to see unique relationships and to optimize their conceptualizing skills may be lost forever.

Teacher shortages are yet another area of concern. The current shortage of qualified teachers in three key areas — math, science, and languages — is projected to worsen dramatically over the next two decades. For lack of a better alternative, some secondary schools have resorted to hiring teachers to teach subjects for which they are less than fully prepared. Finding teachers qualified to teach English as a second language is particularly critical in many locations.

This problem is shared by both rural and urban schools. Often schools cannot afford the luxury of hiring teachers for courses such as trigonometry or Latin if only a few students will enroll. And some schools cannot convince subject-qualified teachers to relocate to their geographic area.

The ongoing dilemma of whether to focus financial and teaching resources on breadth or depth in the curriculum presents yet another problem for the world's schools. Struggling with budget and personnel constraints, many schools must choose between a curriculum that covers a large number of subjects lightly or an intensive, highly focused curriculum that covers key subjects in depth but other areas only superficially, if at all.

This dilemma cuts to the heart of the curriculum reform debate: Will a broad-based, general education or a more focused education (for example, a concentration on math and science) better prepare students for the world they will face as adults?

Proponents for both sides of the debate have presented compelling arguments over the past several years. Most educators still believe the goal is to find a way to offer both breadth and depth, ensuring the most comprehensive educational grounding possible.

INTERNATIONAL PROBLEMS, LOCAL SOLUTIONS

The United States is not alone in its drive for elementary and secondary school reform, but the educational philosophies differ considerably in other countries. As *The Economist* noted in its 1992 report on world education, educational reform has become an international preoccupation:

> The most comprehensive reform programme has been the one implemented by the British government since 1988. This is a mixture of centralization (imposing a national curriculum and reducing the role of local education authorities) and competition (giving schools an incentive to compete for pupils and encouraging pupils to compete for results). This has attracted many imitators and would-be imitators. Sweden is reorganizing its school system into an internal market. Denmark has introduced per-capita funding for technical colleges. Singapore is going for league tables [published competitive rankings] to stimulate competition between schools. American reformers would like to introduce vouchers and national tests. Other reformers are doing just the opposite. In South Korea and Japan the education ministries want to delegate power to local government. The Japanese authorities strongly disapprove of league tables of schools.[13]

Not only is this global concern with reform necessary at all levels of education but it offers a payoff to those on the receiving end, both young students and adult learners. If virtue gets its reward in heaven, education gets its payoff on payday. Learning power is earning power. How to make education affordable and accessible is our next challenge.

[1]Chester E. Finn and Bruno V. Manno, "What's Wrong With the American University," *Wilson Quarterly* 20, No. 1 (Winter 1996): 44–45.

[2]Ibid.

[3]Ibid.

[4]William B. Johnston and Arnold H. Packer, *Workforce 2000: Work and Workers for the Twenty-first Century* (Indianapolis, Ind.: Hudson Institute, 1987), 103.

[5]William Bowen and Julie Ann Sosa, *Prospects for Faculty in the Arts and Sciences* (Princeton, N.J.: Princeton University Press, 1989).

[6]See David T. Kearns and Dennis P. Doyle, *Winning the Brain Race: A Bold Plan to Make Our Schools Competitive* (San Francisco: ICS Press, 1988), 1–14; Jack E. Bowsher, *Education America: Lessons Learned in the Nation's Corporations* (New York: John Wiley & Sons, Inc., 1989), 13–44; and Marvin Cetron and Thomas O'Toole, *Encounters With the Future: A Forecast of Life Into the 21st Century* (New York: McGraw-Hill, 1982), 253–271. Note also the statement by United Auto Workers economist Daniel Laria: "Resisting automation is probably a lower route to employment than accepting it." (Ibid., 267).

[7]World Development Bank, *World Education Report 1995* (Washington, D.C., 1995), 39.

[8]Wilson P. Dizard, Jr., *The Coming Knowledge Age: An Overview of Technology, Economics, and Politics, Third Edition* (New York: Longman Inc., 1989), 97–105.

[9]Tom Peters, *Thriving on Chaos: Handbook for a Management Revolution* (New York: Harper & Row, 1987), 5.

[10]Johnston and Packer, *Workforce 2000*, xxvi–xxvii.

[11]Ibid., 96–97.

[12]United States Congress, Office of Technology Assessment, *Linking for Learning: A New Course for Education*, ITA-SET-430 (Washington, D.C.: U.S. Government Printing Office, November 1989), 27–28.

[13]"A Survey of Education," *The Economist*, 28 November 1992.

**Each person should be able to access
high quality learning opportunities
appropriate to their needs throughout
their life. They should be able to do
this from home, the work place, local
community-based centers, or through
educational institutions.**

— Vision statement:
Open Learning Agency,
British Columbia, Canada

DISTANCE EDUCATION:
THE ROOTS OF CYBERSCHOOLS

Distance education is part of the answer to the quest for affordable, accessible higher education.

Distance education has graduated from its roots in mail-order correspondence courses, in their own day both innovative and democratizing, to become an exciting, effective way to learn. It can employ almost every communications technology application that was developed in the 20th century, be it a TV course, courseware, on-line instruction, an Internet class, or a virtual campus.

Distance education via electronic instruction won't solve all of the world's educational delivery problems, but it can help. If developed wisely and with the combined efforts of the public and private sectors throughout the world, distance education will use increasingly available communications technology to bring education to the learner. That learner can be in the United States or Europe or anywhere on the globe where the Internet is accessible via satellite transmissions, old copper wiring or new fiber links, and computers and TVs or where various convergent combinations forming electronic platforms are available.

THE MEDIUM ISN'T THE MESSAGE

Much of my life has been devoted to the development and deployment of communications tools for the public at large. During that process, I have found that distance education is an instance in which the late media philosopher Marshall McLuhan's (www.utoronto.ca/site/content_marshall.html) maxim, "The medium is the message,"[1] stated in his seminal work, *Understanding Media*, should not be taken literally.

Though communications technology often fascinates us, the content it conveys — education, entertainment, news, and the like — was and still is king. Striving for human interaction to understand, interpret, and debate that content just happens to consume most of our lives. McLuhan's later work, *The Medium Is the Massage*,[2] spelled out in more graphic terms how technology can shape our perception of content. This undeniable phenomenon is the driving force behind much of the concern and debate over education and technology and is addressed in later chapters.

A BRIEF HISTORY

Historical context is useful in understanding the evolution of distance education from its text-based, correspondence course beginnings to its current foundation in technology. Early examples of distance education are generally attributed to the late 19th century, when formal correspondence courses were developed. But the first distance learner to receive full university credit probably did so in the 18th century, when a homebound student on a remote agricultural estate made informal arrangements with a university lecturer to receive course notes and textbooks by mail and completed examinations in writing. The lecturer likely pocketed an "incentive" fee from the student, and university officials were never aware the student on the class roll was a phantom.

As social, demographic, and economic changes shaped both the 19th and 20th centuries, some leaders in education worked to fashion new ways to bring education to those who wanted it. The single most outstanding higher education advancement in 19th century America was U.S. President Abraham Lincoln's 1862 signing of the Morrill Act, which initiated development of a system of state-supported universities intended to make college education more affordable and available to U.S. citizens. The act provided a 19th century bricks-and-mortar solution to the education distribution dilemma in one part of the world. The 1887 Hatch Act established agricultural experiment stations, followed in 1914 by the Smith-Lever Act, which authorized county extension agents for agriculture and home economics. These were some of the first attempts to take education directly from state universities to adult learners in the United States. Today, arguably, the most successful efforts to bring higher education to more people at affordable costs involve distance education.

Initially, telecourses, or televised instruction, proved to be one of the most promising of the technology-based distance education alternatives. Advances in communications technologies such as cable television, fiber optics, microwave, wireless telecommunications systems, satellites, microcomputer networks, fax machines, videocassette recorders, and the Internet have allowed telecourse and courseware design and delivery to become even more effective. Useful electronic tools will continue to evolve.

Beginning in the mid-1990s, the rapid evolution and adaptation of the Internet with its graphical and interactive World Wide Web provided an immediate distance learning medium that distance teaching institutions have been quick to employ. High-speed cable TV modems capable of delivering TV broadcast and Internet services, telephone lines with supercharged asymmetric digital subscriber line (ADSL) or integrated services digital network (ISDN) service, and satellite transmissions beamed directly to homes with telephone and Internet return links are now well established as viable infrastructure for delivery of distance education. The technology, I believe, holds the potential to turn every living room on the globe into a real-time, interactive classroom.

WORLDWIDE DISTANCE HIGHER EDUCATION

Educational systems in sparsely populated countries such as Australia, Canada, and the Scandinavian countries have employed distance learning programs largely in the form of by-mail correspondence courses for more than 100 years. Distance education is used effectively in Australian higher education in particular, where seven universities teach at a distance to about 15,000 students, around 10 percent of their total enrollments. In addition there are 29,000 students enrolled in the distance education programs of the

Colleges of Advanced Education and 350,000 in the Technical and Further Education sector.

In many countries traditional higher education institutions collaborate to design and deliver distance education. Examples are Federation Interuniversitaire de L'Enseignement à Distance in France, which coordinates distance education centers at 22 universities, and Italy's Consorzio Per L'Universita a Distanz, which designs learning materials and support services for students who register with universities that are members of the consortium. In Ontario, Canada, Contact North serves 27 communities through coordinating centers in member colleges and universities.

There also are stand-alone distance learning institutions in more than 20 countries. Many have huge student enrollments. For example, in Thailand the Sukhothai Thammathirat Open University, established in 1978, has some 200,000 students and a goal of admitting around 500,000. Established in the early 1980s and offering more than 500 courses a year, China's Central Radio and Television University (CRTVU) is the largest open-learning institution in the world. CRTVU has an annual total enrollment of about 1.5 million students. It offers three-year junior college level programs. Germany's FernUniversitat has a student body of around 30,000.[3] Other distance learning institutions, listed in the order in which they were founded, include:

Open University of South Africa (1951)
British Open University (1969)
Universidad Nacional de Educacion a Distancia, Spain (1972)

Everyman's University, Israel (1974)

Allama Iqbal Open University, Pakistan (1974)

Universidad Estatal a Distancia, Costa Rica (1977)

Universidad Nacional Abierta, Venezuela (1977)

Anadolu University, Turkey (1981)

Open Universiteit, The Netherlands (1981)

Sri Lanka Institute of Distance Education (1981)

Kyongi Open University, Korea (1982)

University of the Air, Japan (1983)

Universitas Terbuka, Indonesia (1984)

Indira Gandhi National Open University, India (1985)

National Open University, Taiwan (1987)

Al Quds Open University, Jordan (1987)

Universidade Aberta, Portugal (1988)

Open Learning Institute of Hong Kong (1989)

The Russian Confederation of Independent States reportedly has some 14 autonomous distance teaching universities.

But it was the United Kingdom's highly innovative British Open University (BOU) that quickly became an international distance education model by making college-level learning available to the general public. This institution truly opened the doors to distance learning and defied the "education for the elite" philosophy that still to a certain extent dominates European higher education systems.

Championed by then Prime Minister Harold Wilson, BOU was created as an alternative system for earning a higher education degree. Its courses blended print, radio, and some video presentations with campus visits. They were designed to appeal to students unable to attend universities full-time or in residence. There were no admission requirements. Anyone could enroll in BOU, but only students who successfully completed course requirements could obtain a degree.

To support its far-flung population, BOU established sites throughout the United Kingdom where students could take exams and meet with tutors. Beginning with an enrollment of 40,000 in 1971, BOU now counts more than 165,000 in its student body. In 1999, the university opened a new campus in the United States. In 1994, it counted 5,000 of its students from the European Union. Another 8,000 students take BOU courses through partnership agreements with institutions in Central and Eastern Europe. One of BOU's largest contributions to distance education is that it helped set the precedent for using radio and television to deliver higher education courses, though it was somewhat slow in providing Internet-based delivery.

TV: EDUCATION DIRECT TO YOUR LIVING ROOM

Telecourses have been part of the U.S. educational delivery system since televised classes were first broadcast into America's homes more than 35 years ago. Typically received by ordinary home antennas from local broadcast television stations, these early, rudimentary telecourses brought traditional classroom presentations directly into students' living rooms.

Chicago Citywide College, an extension of the City College of Chicago, took the lead in testing and developing this new educational delivery system.[4] Supported by a grant from the Ford Foundation's Fund for the Advancement of Education, Chicago Citywide College began broadcasting telecourses over Chicago's public education television station, WTTW, in 1956. From those early days of trial-and-error experimentation, Chicago Citywide College has continued its commitment to expand the applicability and enhance the effectiveness of telecourse instruction. And, although many other colleges have since followed its lead, Chicago Citywide's program is generally recognized to have set the stage for educational television today.

Also in 1956, while Chicago Citywide College was establishing itself, another Ford Foundation–supported project for television in higher education was launched at Pennsylvania State University. The purpose of the Penn State project was to explore the potential of closed-circuit television for on-campus instruction. It was successful. The project had produced 28 courses for the university by 1966.

Beyond closed-circuit courses, the 1950s spawned university-owned and -operated television stations. Examples include KUON, at the University of Nebraska–Lincoln, and WUNC, at the University of North Carolina at Chapel Hill. Many have since developed into highly effective statewide networks.

Widespread experimentation with telecourses continued at U.S. universities through the 1960s, '70s and '80s. Educators at Michigan State University, at East Lansing, American University in Washington, D.C., Case Western Reserve University in Cleveland, Ohio, and Iowa State University in Ames, among others, explored the possibilities offered by instructional television. They worked with a variety of professionals — teachers, instructional designers, graphic artists, educational technologists, and students — to find the most effective ways to create and deliver telecourses.

COMMERCIAL TV'S EARLY FORAYS INTO EDUCATION

Colleges and universities that did not own a station or a closed-circuit system got their opportunity to experiment with television courses when the commercial networks became interested in educational television. WCBS/New York first broadcast New York University's Sunrise Semester series on comparative literature in 1957. By 1958, NBC was broadcasting "Atomic Age Physics" on Continental Classroom over 150 network stations across the country. Funded in part by another grant from the Ford Foundation, the physics series received high marks from educators for academic quality and the usefulness of the accompanying support materials for students and local teachers. More than 300 colleges and universities offered "Atomic Age Physics" the first year, and several other courses followed in succeeding years.

Unfortunately, the series required a heavy subsidy, and NBC dropped it after a few seasons. Nevertheless, educators, programmers, and producers learned valuable lessons about telecourses from the experience. Indeed, they learned that a program created with high academic standards would be accepted by teachers and students; that a market for such programs existed; and that, as always, financial issues needed to be considered. After a 25-year run, NYU's Sunrise Semester was discontinued in 1982.

PUBLIC TELEVISION

Another landmark event for telecourses in the early 1960s was the passage of the Federal Educational Television Facilities Act of 1962. This legislation empowered the federal government to fund the building and equipping of public television stations, thereby extending educational television's broadcast reach.

In response to the growing interest in telecourses, the Great Plains Regional Instructional Library was created in 1963 by an agency of the KUON-TV/Nebraska Educational Television Network in affiliation with the University of Nebraska–Lincoln. The library's goal was to serve as a clearing-house that would acquire, maintain, and lend to schools those programs and series that had continuing educational value.

Headquartered in Lincoln, Nebraska, the library now houses some 2,300 educational programs for elementary, secondary, and higher education and produces the young reader "Reading Rainbow" series for the Public Broadcasting System (PBS).

WATERSHED: THE PUBLIC BROADCASTING ACT OF 1967

Probably the biggest attempt to advance educational television in the United States occurred with the passage of the Public Broadcasting Act of 1967. It recognized the potential of broadcast television to inform and enlighten as well as entertain the public. This legislation authorized the creation of the Corporation for Public Broadcasting (CPB), which was charged with the "responsibility of assisting new stations in getting on the air, establishing one or more systems of interconnection, obtaining grants from federal and other sources, providing funds to support local programming, and conducting research and training projects."[5]

The CPB was not a production or networking facility. PBS was created in 1969 to serve as CPB's television network. Its functions were to select, schedule, and distribute programming for the widespread system of PBS-affiliated stations. Through that network, a nationwide system of public television comprising some 350 local stations came into being.

The question from an educational standpoint is could much of this development have been accomplished more efficiently by outsourcing more of it to the private sector? As an entrepreneur with decades of experience in this field, I think the answer is, was, and will continue to be *yes*. My rationale is explained in greater depth in Chapter 10.

COMMUNITY COLLEGE TV

In the mid-1970s, community colleges began producing their own telecourse series and related support materials to attract broader audiences and extend the reach of their campuses. Miami–Dade Community College in Miami, Florida, Coastline Community College District in Fountain Valley, California, and Dallas County Community College in Dallas, Texas, were three of the colleges most active in this field. Since then, many community colleges have joined together in regional consortiums that currently produce some of the best telecourse programs available throughout the world.

ANNENBERG/CPB AND THE STAR SCHOOLS PROGRAM

The 1980s produced an explosion of alternative instructional delivery systems for public elementary, secondary, and higher education in America. Fueling major research and experimentation during this period was former Ambassador to Great Britain Walter Annenberg's establishment in 1981 of the landmark Annenberg/ CPB Project, through which the Annenberg School of Communications at the University of Pennsylvania contracted to provide $10 million a year for 15 years to CPB.

The goal of the project was to expand opportunities for people to acquire a quality college education at an affordable cost. To that end, the project supported the development of a collection of telecourses that could be offered to students at more convenient times and places than the traditional classroom hours. It also funded demonstrations of new applications of the telecommunication and information technologies in higher education. The purpose of this funding was to explore improvements in education made possible by advances in technology.[6]

Subsequently, the federal government took a more active role in exploring — and funding — distance education. Perhaps the most ambitious undertaking so far is the federal government's Star Schools Program for elementary and secondary schools. Created by the Omnibus Trade Bill and Competitive Act in 1988, the Star Schools Program was designed to address "critical needs in the rebuilding of our education system to meet domestic and international challenges."

The priorities of the Star Schools Program were "to create multistate, organizationally diverse partnerships to write and deliver both core and enrichment curriculum, and to create opportunities for disadvantaged students to receive remote instruction."[7] By insisting on multistate, multi-institutional partnerships, the bill's authors hoped to encourage new ways for the nation's remotely located and under-served students to gain access to quality education. Distance education technology has been the central vehicle for achieving this goal.

The Star Schools Program was authorized as a five-year program with an overall funding limit of $100 million. In pursuit of this goal, Congress appropriated $33.5 million over a two-year period to ensure that U.S. students had "access to basic and advanced courses in mathematics, science, and foreign languages."[8]

Four projects were selected for the first two-year grant period, three satellite-delivered projects and one based on a combination of computers and telecommunications. At this writing, Star Schools' funding had been renewed and prospects for continued federal funding were good.

However, programs so critically important to students in the knowledge age should not have to live or die depending upon the vagaries of Congressional funding priorities. I believe Star Schools should try to find a way to stand on its own. Indeed, with the future possibility of shrinking government coffers, most publicly funded entities should be creating alternative, private-sector survival plans – it's an exercise in self-sustainability. History indicates that often when public funding ends, so does the project.

As we enter the 21st century, our challenge will be to build on the insights and experiences gained in the past four decades. These advances have created unprecedented opportunities to tailor education to the needs of students, rather than having students structure their education around the needs of institutions.

With broad-scale ability to become educated comes broad-scale opportunity — economic and otherwise. With recognizable opportunity and broad-scale access to it comes a broad-scale sense of fairness and hope. I believe a sense of fairness and a hopeful attitude are positive elements that our world society needs. They are confidence-builders personally, organizationally, nationally, and globally.

[1]Marshall McLuhan, *Understanding Media: The Extensions of Man* (New York: New American Library, 1964), 23.

[2]Marshall McLuhan and Quentin Fiore, *The Medium Is the Massage: An Inventory of Effects* (New York: Bantam Books, 1967), 26.

[3]Barbara L. Watkins and Stephen J. Wright, *The Foundation of American Distance Education: A Century of Collegiate Correspondence Study* (Dubuque, Iowa: Kendall/Hunt Publishing Company, 1991), 199, 295, 297.

[4]Michael G. Moore and Melody M. Thompson, *The Effects of Distance Learning: A Summary of Literature* (University Park, Pa.: The American Center for the Study of Distance Education, 1990), 3.

[5]D. N. Wood and D. G. Wylie, "Reaching New Students Through New Technologies," *Educational Telecommunications* (Belmont, Calif.: Wadsworth Publishing Company, 1977), 33.

[6]Annenberg/CPB project statement, 1987.

[7]United States Congress, Office of Technology Assessment, *Linking for Learning: A New Course for Education*, ITA-SET-430 (Washington, D.C.: U.S. Government Printing Office, November 1989), 136.

[8]U.S. Senate Committee on Labor and Human Resources, *The Star Schools Program Assistance Act of 1987*, 100th Cong., 1st sess., 1987, S. Rept. 100-44, 1.

The Virtual Classroom is one of those things that is best experienced, like a sunset swim in ocean waves, in order to fully understand it.

— Starr Roxanne Hiltz,
in *The Virtual Classroom*

THE VIRTUAL CLASSROOM OF THE 21ST CENTURY

The days when the overhead projector was the highest-tech teaching tool to grace the halls of ivy are over. The numbers prove it. For example, in 1994 e-mail was used in only 8 percent of college courses in the United States. By 1999, that percentage had soared to 54 percent. In 1996, only 9.2 percent of college courses had Web pages. In 1999, the number had almost tripled to 28.1 percent. A modest beginning, but, as Kenneth Green, director of the U.S. Annual Campus Computing Survey, wrote in an issue of *Change* magazine, "Most colleges and universities have finally passed the point of critical mass affecting the instructional use of information technology."

Technology doesn't necessarily have to come in the form of a microcomputer. For technophobic teachers, perhaps just an Internet access device would suffice. But the higher education establishment must adapt to technology in the lecture hall or perhaps even get used to technology *as* the lecture hall. A true paradigm shift needs to occur in the way college educators and the higher education establishment perceive and design the education environment.

Equally important, technology can be used to create a less expensive way to deliver higher education to those who want it. Although there will never be a substitute for the experience of the college campus, advances in computers, cable television, and satellite technology and the ubiquitousness of the Internet and its World Wide Web will make higher education available to the most people at the lowest cost — worldwide.

In 1996, in the first edition of this book, I predicted that the dawning of the 21st century would usher in the full use of technology-based institutions that could function side by side with traditional universities. This has come about as a number of universities around the world — including Stanford, Harvard, MIT, University of Colorado, and many, many others — have gone on-line with a variety of degree and certificate programs that offer the same credentials to their graduates as their campus-based counterparts.

In spring 1999, the North Central Association of Colleges and Schools, one of the six key accrediting bodies for higher education in the United States, granted accreditation to Jones International University (JIU) for bachelor's and master's degrees in business communications. JIU, which my company founded and operates, was the first purely virtual higher education institution to achieve this status. In spring 2000, JIU also received accreditation for its Master's in Business Administration program.

THE LIVING ROOM AS CLASSROOM

The idea is to deliver education to people, instead of people to education. The idea is to deliver education to the living room, whether that living room is in Alabama or Argentina. Why now? Because, as we all know, earning a living in post-industrial, knowledge-age society requires lifelong learning, training, and retraining at every level. For the vast majority, interrupting work life to study in a traditional university setting is out of the question.

What does "virtual" mean? The term virtual is used in computer science to refer to something whose existence is simulated with software, rather than actually existing in some physical form.

The virtual university is education dispensed from an electronic platform, instead of a lecture hall podium. Indeed, work on virtual classrooms and virtual universities has been taking place since the 1980s, both in the private sector and in the public sector at university consortia, governors' conferences, and public television studios.

Since 1996, the rapid evolution of new software standards, and particularly the recognition of the World Wide Web as an open software platform, has led to major shakeups and shifts in the development of educational delivery software and standards by major technology companies. In 1996, Apple Computer, Inc., was creating a proprietary software/hardware/network package called the Apple Virtual Campus.[1] By late 1999, that project had largely been leapfrogged by the company's strategic shift to recognizing a variety of Web tools that allow students, faculty, and administrators to create their own content using Internet browsers and such multimedia software as Apple's QuickTime. As with competing educational delivery providers, Apple's goals remained the same: allowing students, faculty, and administrators at a university to be able to record, send, and receive information from any location to any other location at any moment in time.

Sun Microsystem's development of Java open-programming tools has both accelerated and eased the migration of education onto the Internet. Although Sun has developed proprietary distance educational delivery software and hardware for customers, its shift toward a Web standard has also been notable.

The world-renowned British Open University (BOU) in the United Kingdom used Sun's Java software to develop a program called Stadium, which is designed to allow thousands of students at a time to listen to and participate in special guest lectures given on the university's virtual campus. Stadium's creators tout it as an experiment in "very large telepresence." Telepresence captures the mood of an event — applause, laughter, shouting, whispers between neighbors, and the like — using software.

BOU is also making millennium-level shifts in its strategies by moving more of its courses from television delivery to CD-ROMs and the Internet. In one of its most momentous ventures ever, BOU has opened a satellite "campus" via the Internet with courses aimed specifically at American students.

VIRTUAL CLASSROOMS: BETTER THAN REAL?

For the uninitiated the concept is a little tough to grasp. But, as virtual classroom design innovator Starr Roxanne Hiltz, head of the Computer Assisted Learning Program at the New Jersey Institute of Technology, advises,

> The virtual classroom is one of those things that is best experienced, like a sunset swim in ocean waves, in order to fully understand it…think of all the different kinds of learning tools and spaces and ritualized forms of interaction that take place within a traditional classroom and within an entire college campus or high school. All of these things exist within a virtual classroom, too, except that all of the activities and interactions are mediated by computer software, rather than by face-to-face interaction.[2]

First introduced in the mid-1980s, Hiltz's technology was used by the ConnectEd, or Connected Education, program, part of the New School University in New York City, to link instructors in North America with students in Asia, Europe, and Latin America.[3] The technology was used much like the Internet is used today: A student in Asia could dial a local telephone number to connect with the mainframe computer in New Jersey to receive any course material stored there, to leave or receive papers, or to communicate with an instructor or other class members.

Another way to think about the virtual classroom is to compare it with how interaction takes place in a traditional classroom. In traditional classrooms, most interaction takes place via speaking, listening, reading, and writing. In the virtual classroom, interaction takes place entirely by typing and reading from a computer terminal. If that seems like a less than superior alternative to the traditional classroom, it really is not. Hiltz contends a collaborative learning environment that is computer mediated can support some activities that are difficult or impossible to conduct in face-to-face environments, particularly if there is a large class. In the virtual classroom, discussion and communication about the course become a continuous activity. If a student has an idea or a question, it can be communicated while it is fresh.

The advantages of the virtual university's being virtually anywhere — in a living room, a kitchen corner, or the local library — are obvious, but I'll list them anyway: All students in a particular class don't have to be at the same place at the same time, week after week, for the course of a semester; and the virtual university is open 24 hours a day, seven days a week. For adult learners with jobs and family responsibilities, the ability to do coursework on their own schedules may make the difference between successfully completing a degree program and dropping out.

If you think about using traditional terms, in the virtual university interaction "spaces" are created within a software package and are used as so-called classrooms, where teachers lecture and where group discussions take place; there is a communication structure like office hours, through which student and teacher can communicate privately. The software also has the ability to administer, collect, and grade tests or assignments and the ability to divide a larger class into smaller working or peer groups for collaborative assignments.[4]

All this happens within a computer-mediated communication system. Two examples are the local area network, through which students and teachers can communicate via electronic bulletin boards, e-mail, private news groups on the Internet (also called list-servs), and private chat rooms. The local area network by its nature can restrict the virtual classroom to a certain defined area, like a college campus, and a course delivered over the Internet's World Wide Web can have a similar structure with password restrictions.

The concept has been tested and is successful. As of early 2000, more than 70,000 courses worldwide were being offered partly or completely via the Internet.

Virtual Education Visions

One of the latest virtual education visions comes from the governors of several states in the western United States. They have created an institution in cyberspace called Western Governors' University. In early 2000, it offered five technology-related degree programs and courses from another 47 higher education institutions and was a candidate for accreditation. The governors first discussed their virtual university idea at the Western Governors' Association's annual meeting in June 1995 in Park City, Utah. Money, as often is the case in both government and the private sector, was the driver. The concept grew out of a discussion about how to contain the costs of producing expensive distance learning courses and the states' limited capacity to fund increasingly expensive traditional higher education. What evolved was a vision for a combination of technology and face-to-face modes — specifically, cable television, Internet-based courses, and summer seminars — delivering education to far-flung students in all the idyllic nooks and crannies of this sparsely populated region.

The governors' objectives mirror those of many other distance learning programs. Their goals are similar, too, in that they mention extending educational opportunities to more citizens, reducing the costs of higher education, and shifting the focus of education away from "seat time" and toward competence.[5]

I have one more goal to suggest to the governors (one that the tenor of their proposal clearly embraces), and that is to truly make the student the focus of the process, not the institution or the teacher.

The governors claim their virtual university is an alternative concept for U.S. higher education, with learning delivered to students on campus, at home, in libraries, or at work. We know the concept works. In the United States alone, National Technological University, Coastline Community College, and more than 70 other U.S. universities and colleges have a wealth of experience in delivering electronic, accredited courses that can be referred to for guidance and expertise.

THE VIRTUAL LIBRARY

We have known that, since the beginning of civilization, knowledge is power. Dating back to the end of the Middle Ages, at the heart of every traditional university has been a great library.

Indeed, in the early 17th century, Sir Francis Bacon may have created one of the first library cataloguing systems. As part of his essay, *In Advancement of Learning*, he divided "all knowledge" according to the faculties of memory, imagination, and reason — complete with subdivisions. In the knowledge age, we have taken the vision of the great library further: At the heart of the great virtual university is a great virtual library. There is enough digital and digitized information today to develop virtual libraries filled with the world's knowledge and available to anyone with access to a computer and a modem. Think about it: on-line access to the globe's important information by every scholar in the world.

Here are a few examples: The University of California at Berkeley's Digital Library Project (sunsite.berkeley.edu) has digitized a large array of collections now accessible to the public. The collections vary from aerial photography to medieval and early Renaissance manuscripts, the Jack London Collection, the Icelandic Genome project, and many more. Meanwhile, the University of California at Santa Barbara is working on the Alexandria Digital Library, which ultimately will create full-content search-and-retrieval video libraries, and the University of Illinois is building a large-scale digital library with the goal of bringing professional quality search-and-display capability to Internet information services. The University of Michigan and Stanford University also are working on digital libraries.

In fact, almost every major university research library in the United States has initiated a program to place part of its collections and archives into digital format, usually available for free on the World Wide Web. A similar spontaneous movement is taking place in Europe and parts of Asia, as evidenced by the Treasures of Europe's National Libraries collection on the Web, the Bibliothèque Nationale de la France's program to digitize thousands of French texts and images, and the University of Adelaide's Electronic Text Collection.

All these projects are aiming toward something entirely new: the management of digital as well as digitized information. As Paul Evan Peters, executive director of the Coalition of Networked Information, describes it:

> The knowledge objects enabled by this emergent class of digital libraries will be much more like "experience" than they will be like things, much more like programs than documents, and readers will have unique experiences with these objects in an even more profound way than is already the case with books, periodicals, etc.[6]

This is the virtual library of the future. Governments the world over would do well to fund the creation of new digitized and digital content and leave the building of telecommunications infrastructure to deliver it to users to the private sector.

JONES'S VIRTUAL LIBRARY IN CYBERSPACE

Using the wealth of Internet-based information resources available today from such sources as the U.S. Library of Congress, national and international agencies and associations, governments, and scholars across the globe, JonesKnowledge.com has created a virtual library in cyberspace: the *e*-global Library™ (www.jones. com/egl.html). This virtual collection, password-accessible for JIU students and other *e*-global Library clients via the World Wide Web, highlights the best of the digitized library resources around the world. You could say it serves as a "cybrarian" for the students of the virtual university and the knowledge age. Among the library's offerings are a collection of more than 2,500 Internet-based academic resources (updated monthly), guides to libraries and how to use them for research, a guide to the Internet as a research tool, more than 50 unique research guides on core academic and business topics, and on-call reference assistance. All have been prepared for Internet access, and all are rich research resources, delivered directly to the student or client.

Soon more digitized resources will be available. The Library of Congress's National Digital Library Program (http://lcweb.loc.gov/ bicentennial/digital.html), under the outstanding leadership of its librarian, Dr. James Billington, planned to digitize some 5 million items by the end of 2000. This is the largest repository of information in the world. Congress allocated $3 million a year from 1996 to 2001 for the project. Congress also has requested that The Library of Congress raise $3 of private funding for every dollar of public funding allocated to the project. To that end, corporate and individual contributions have come from John Kluge, the David and Lucile Packard Foundation, the W.W. Kellogg Foundation, Ameritech, Bell Atlantic Corporation, the McCormick Tribune Foundation, The Discovery Channel, Eastman Kodak Company, Reuters, Compaq

Computer Corporation, The Hearst Foundation, R.R. Donnelly & Sons, NYNEX Corporation, and Nortel. Total funding as of 2000 for the project was more than $60 million.

THE U.K. COLLECTION

In the United Kingdom, a massive effort called the Electronic Libraries Programme has been undertaken by a consortium of universities with $15 million in funding. U.K. universities are digitizing vast collections of 18th and 19th century journals such as *Gentleman's Magazine, The Annual Registry, Philosophical Transactions of the Royal Society*, and many more. Anyone with access to the Internet will be able to peruse these collections on their desktops. Also being digitized are journals in design and applied arts. Though CD-ROM may be the best method of delivery for these journals, delivery via the Internet is also possible.

The U.K. program also may use on-demand publishing — a way to deliver electronically stored materials to more students at a time. Archivists are interested in developing flexible licensing arrangements for multiple sets of copyrighted materials to be printed and handed out for student use.

Copyright laws are a sticky issue in the world of digitization and virtual electronic libraries. Currently, documents not considered to be in what is called the public domain are subject to copyright laws. Libraries and other institutions that want to put copyrighted material on the World Wide Web or other electronic bulletin board systems still must get permission from the materials' authors or their estates. Music is a particular problem because so many different entities — composers, record companies, publishers — all have rights to the material.

ANOTHER ON-LINE OPTION

For students who can't wait for all the world's knowledge to be recorded in 1s and 0s, a nondigitized worldwide library project is the On-line Computer Library Center, Inc. (OCLC), headquartered near Columbus, Ohio. It is the world's largest bibliographic computer system. In 2000, it was serving more than 30,000 libraries in 65 countries, including the database of Kinki University Library in Osaka, Japan. Information does not have to be digitized to be catalogued in this center, but OCLC now has an extensive digitization project on the Web (www.oclc.org). This project includes many of OCLC's electronic journal materials, as well as reciprocal links to its member libraries along with their catalogs and their own digitized collections.

It is hoped that as more and more rare, classical literary artifacts become digitized and available to living room–based patrons of virtual libraries, educational barriers that divide societies will begin to crumble. I believe these libraries in cyberspace will become to the 21st century what the fax machine was to the late 20th century. Information disseminated by fax helped change the world's political balance when the Iron Curtain collapsed in the late 1980s. Wouldn't it be wonderful if in the 21st century the ability to share the world's knowledge through virtual libraries and global virtual universities brought the world to the next level of understanding? It can happen.

TEACHERS AS HOLOGRAMS?

Despite the evidence, there are arguments in traditional educational circles that virtual universities, classrooms, and libraries lack the synergism of the traditional delivery systems and that students will, therefore, learn less. Understandably, professors appearing as holograms is a discomfiting idea. I can understand why these entrenched opinions exist, but I urge their proponents to rethink them.

Here's why. In the virtual classroom, it is virtually impossible to be a passive learner. Students nearly always must react or provide some appropriate input in order to continue to the next phase of an assignment. In addition, virtual courses are more often designed to be collaborative efforts among students than are the traditional lecture hall courses we all knew and loved — at least for the sheer anonymity they provided.

All mediums of communication have their advantages and disadvantages. But the research really does show there is no significant difference in the student's ability to learn using technology-based educational tools — and not just for computer-aided teaching. Long ago, research into whether television was an inferior learning tool proved there is no real difference between learning from TV and the Internet and learning in the traditional classroom.[7] Researchers and academicians debate the pros and cons of virtual classrooms, but most early indicators are that the same is true for education via computers and the Internet. And with 7 million students working full time in the United States alone,[8] there certainly is a market for virtual universities to tap.

At the beginning of any paradigm shift — and the knowledge age is demanding a paradigm shift in educational delivery — there must be explorers. The technology available today plus the current economics of higher education demand that we either become adventurers ourselves or provide the opportunity for others to be.

---

[1]Author unknown, "Apple America's Higher Education: A Vision Shared," April 16, 1996, www.apple.com/technology.html.

[2]Starr Roxanne Hiltz, *The Virtual Classroom* (Norwood, N.J.: Ablex Publishing Corporation, 1994), 4.

[3]Parker Rossman, *The Emerging Worldwide Electronic University: Knowledge Age Global Higher Education* (Westport, Conn.: Greenwood Press, 1992), 46–47.

[4]Hiltz, *Virtual Classroom*, 6.

[5]Western Governors' Association, *From Vision to Reality: A Western Virtual University* (Denver, Colo., 1996), 1.

[6]Paul Evan Peters, "Digital Libraries Are Much More Than Digitized Collections," *Educom Review*, July–August 1995.

[7]Hiltz, *Virtual Classroom*, 20.

[8]Robert Moskowitz, "Wired U," *Internet World*, October 1995, 60.

It appears that [television] is at least on the verge of fulfilling the great hope of the 1940s — that each home could be a university center as long as it had a television set and a willing learner.

5

> — Dee Brock,
> Former Director of Adult
> Learning Programming,
> Public Broadcasting System,
> United States

JONESKNOWLEDGE.COM™: AN ENTREPRENEURIAL APPROACH

Dee Brock wrote the words above in 1985, when she was Director of Adult Learning Programming at the Public Broadcasting System. That was two years before Jones International launched its cable television educational programming channel, Mind Extension University, the predecessor to JonesKnowledge.com.

By the early 1990s, Mind Extension University had made the living room a potential university classroom for at least 26 million cable television subscribers and satellite dish owners in the United States, for viewers of cable and satellite television in various Asian countries including Thailand, China, and Taiwan, and for countries in the European Union.

TV'S IMPACT

For distance education, television arguably was the transforming technology of the 20th century. The opening of the ultra-high-frequency spectrum in the 1960s and 1970s, which brought the explosive growth of noncommercial television stations, plus the advent of cable TV brought educational programming home, so to speak.

As anyone who had the experience of sitting through an early TV course well knows, televised courses were not polished at first. Indeed, Brock notes, "The camera was just an observer sitting in the front row"[1] of a college classroom. Televised courses often were broadcast only on closed-circuit TV or microwave to other classrooms on campus. Times have changed. Although the TV medium of educational delivery is still quite viable, it is rapidly being replaced by the migration of distance learning systems to the Internet. If you have never seen an example of an electronically delivered college course, do yourself a favor and click on Jones-Knowledge.com through your computer's browser. Check out the guest section of the site for Jones International University (JIU) at www.jonesinternational.edu and see a sampling of what students are doing at both the bachelor's and master's levels of instruction.

The Web-based course is learner-focused to engage students in a way that 250-seat lecture halls have never been able to achieve. It is not a traditional lecture format, and it involves more than a professor dumping course notes onto a page of hyper-text markup language (HTML). Students are encouraged to read text and do class preparation off-line, then be prepared to spend time engaged in discussion with the lecturer and classmates. As appropriate, multimedia — such as video and audio streaming — are used to promote learning.

Typically this is done in an asynchronous, or variable-time interval. Interaction is designed to promote learning and to build a sense of community between faculty and students, among students, and among faculty members. Interaction takes the form of discussion and debate, whereby the professor or faculty member initiates a conversation via computer using the discussion feature of the course software.

Each participant's contributions to the discussion or answers to individual questions are threaded, meaning each participant's responses are tagged and linked together. All participants can immediately identify and review an individual's total contribution to the discussion and the entire class's responses to a particular question or topic, usually by date and time. Individual students can initiate a question for the teacher or for other students using the same feature. Spontaneous discussions among individuals or small groups can happen any time of the day or night, with the results recorded for the rest of the class to review later. This is a true collaborative learning environment, in which individuals from around the world work on group projects with a real-world orientation.

This method of interaction allows the faculty member to engage students around the globe in learning because it mitigates the problems caused by different time zones. Students may go on-line at different times to make their comments, or they may opt to go on-line at the same time as the instructor and other class members and see the questions and comments appear in real time. The instructor sets the deadlines by which contributions or responses must be completed. From the student's standpoint, this method is extremely convenient because the work can be accessed at a time

Endicott College
Beverly, Mass. 01915

when he or she is ready to learn, whether it is midnight or noon. From the teacher's perspective, the method can be used to require every student to participate, and there is an immediate record of the participation. Nobody can hide or avoid contributing.

Course notes, class add-ons, and appendixes are "hyperlinked," taking each member of the course to electronic resources or an electronic library such as Jones's *e*-global Library,™ which has placed on-line or located and organized thousands of relevant resources for the courses offered. By means of digital cameras and transmissions, lecturers and students can take field trips, observe laboratory experiments, or interview professional experts at their work sites, either live or delayed.

And this is all available worldwide, wherever there is access to a computer with at least a 28.8 baud modem and an Internet Service Provider hookup. Like the TV courses they have replaced, Internet courses can enhance a student's learning experience visually and graphically. This has been one of the seminal technology applications of the knowledge age.

EXTENDING THE HUMAN MIND

JonesKnowledge.com is in the business of extending the human mind. JonesKnowledge.com is a proactive, entrepreneurial effort to empower the individual through education and thus to contribute to the conversion of information into knowledge, understanding, and wisdom. The company provides solutions that overcome the barriers of time, distance, and, to some extent, economics.

I believe JonesKnowledge.com is not only a part of the evolution of the Internet and television but also of the evolution of education itself. The company has created an environment in which viewers' minds are actively engaged, vast amounts of information can be delivered inexpensively, and distance is erased.

In its initial phase in November 1987, the company began a basic cable television channel designed to meet diverse needs for education, information, and instruction. Equally important in this age of skyrocketing tuition costs, JonesKnowledge.com's original mission included reducing the cost of higher education degrees. As Tables 6 and 7 show, JonesKnowledge.com is still making good on its pledge.

Today JonesKnowledge.com's Internet delivery platform offers for-credit, college-level courses in science, fine arts, English, mathematics, foreign languages, health care, general business, computing, and the Internet, including certificate programs in most of these disciplines. It is also becoming the platform of choice for a variety of K–12 educational offerings. It is a leader in the development and deployment of e-learning solutions for corporations, as well as educational institutions, worldwide. Courses are including more video material as greater consumer access to broadbrand Internet delivery makes it possible to transmit streaming full-motion video to students' home and office computer workstations.

In essence, JonesKnowledge.com wants to reach the hundreds of thousands who want higher education degrees and certificates for professional development or to supplement a K–12 curriculum. It's perfectly all right to sign up for one, two, or three courses just to brush up on communication or Internet skills, for example, or to take a corporate training course module.

The target audience is learners with limited time who need a flexible educational option that they can balance with their personal and professional lives. The option also offers high-quality content and affordability.

JONESKNOWLEDGE.COM'S CONTENT PROVIDERS

JonesKnowledge.com is essentially a public/private partnership. Currently dozens of affiliate universities, colleges, companies, and other educational providers across the United States, including Jones International University (JIU), use the company's *e*-education™ course software and related services to deliver distance courses over the Internet. Students can take part or, in some cases, all of their degree requirements without spending time on campus.

For example, on the community college level, Seattle Central Community College offers an associate of arts degree using *e*-education software. Courses are equivalent to freshman and sophomore offerings at four-year institutions and are designed to transfer to four-year bachelor's degree programs. In addition, the Colorado Online School Consortium, a group of K–12 schools in the state, uses the *e*-education software and services of JonesKnowledge.com to provide certain courses to students whose budget and distance constraints would otherwise make taking coursework impossible.

JonesKnowledge.com is the business service provider and does not hand out diplomas. Students receive their degree from the institution that is providing their particular degree program. Accordingly, if they take their courses from Seattle Central, they get their degrees from that institution. If they take their courses from JIU, it awards their degree. In both instances, *e*-education software is the common thread.

For both educational institutions and corporate clients, JonesKnowledge.com offers a supply chain of optional services, including: consultation; instructional design; skills assessment and mapping; catalog, registration, and payment; delivery of content; records and reports; support services; educational resource integration; and on-line resources, such as the *e*-global Library. All are provided via custom portal Web sites, designed for individual clients.

JONESKNOWLEDGE.COM'S CYBERFAMILY

The Jones educational cyberfamily began in 1987 as the cable TV channel called Mind Extension University. Its telecourses were delivered primarily through sister company Jones Intercable, Inc., and via other cable and satellite delivery systems in North and South America, Europe, and Asia. In 1993, the company founded JIU and began developing its own proprietary Internet-based software. This software was initially used in conjunction with the telecourse delivery. Through the mid-1990s, students usually had the option of taking at least part of their coursework via computer, though there was still a heavy reliance on TV-based video delivery.

As the Internet gained popularity and became the technology of choice for many students, Jones decided to fully implement an Internet-based educational delivery system. JIU became the test bed for the company's software and for the development of administrative procedures and services to aid both JIU and JonesKnowledge.com's client universities and companies. JIU was the first purely on-line "cyber" university to receive regional accreditation. The accreditation is identical to that conferred on most traditional bricks-and-mortar universities.

As explained in Chapter 4, JIU is accredited by the North Central Association of Colleges and Schools, the U.S. regional accreditation body that accredits traditional colleges and universities in the Midwest and Rocky Mountain region, where Jones is headquartered.

In 1999, Jones Intercable, Inc., was sold to Comcast Corp. of Philadelphia, the third largest cable system operator in the United States. A portion of the proceeds from that sale were used to finance the further development of *e*-education software, JIU, and other JonesKnowledge.com activities.

In 2000, JIU offered a fully accredited master's in business administration (MBA) with seven specializations, a master's in business communication, a bachelor's completion program in business communication, and a variety of business certificate programs, including a number developed in collaboration with corporate partners. Several additional degree programs and specializations were in the development stages. Using JonesKnowledge.com services and software, client universities and corporations offer a wider variety of courses including MBAs, nursing completion degrees, and classes in hotel and restaurant management, accounting, general studies, computer science, and engineering. The virtual campuses for the students enrolled in these degree programs and individual courses don't have football teams or dormitories. They do have top-quality courses taught in an accelerated format with content provided by some of the finest minds at prestigious universities and community colleges.

Courses are taught in English; however, in mid-2000, the company began experimenting with offering help screens and e-mail assistance in other languages, beginning with Spanish. Students came from 44 countries and all U.S. states. Course content has been developed by experts at such major universities as Carnegie-Mellon, Columbia, Depauw, Georgetown, Indiana, London Business School, London School of Economics and Political Science, Louisiana State, Michigan State, Purdue, Simon Fraser, Thunderbird, Tulane, University of Alabama, University of California, University of Colorado, University of Denver, University of Houston, University of Illinois, University of North Carolina, University of Oklahoma, University of Pittsburgh, University of Southern California, and the University of Texas.

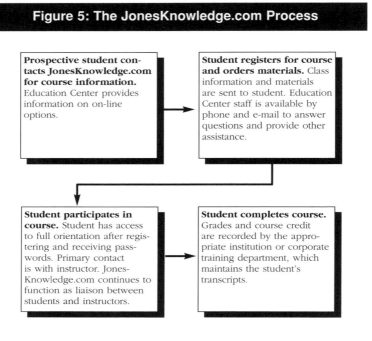

Figure 5: The JonesKnowledge.com Process

Prospective student contacts JonesKnowledge.com for course information. Education Center provides information on on-line options.

Student registers for course and orders materials. Class information and materials are sent to student. Education Center staff is available by phone and e-mail to answer questions and provide other assistance.

Student participates in course. Student has access to full orientation after registering and receiving passwords. Primary contact is with instructor. Jones-Knowledge.com continues to function as liaison between students and instructors.

Student completes course. Grades and course credit are recorded by the appropriate institution or corporate training department, which maintains the student's transcripts.

How a Jones Education Works

The process by which students can take classes through JIU is illustrated in Figure 5. Courses also come from partner/client institutions that license the proprietary Web-based software, *e*-education, and deliver their own courses or have an agreement for Jones Knowledge.com to assist in the preparation and delivery of their courses. The *e*-education platform is complete, offering students and clients a full range of registrar, faculty, and student support services, including 24-hour, seven-day-a-week technology and academic hotlines and e-mail help; basic Internet tutoring; testing; Web course preparation, tutoring, and advising; and a range of additional services. JIU uses the full complement of *e*-education software and services. Client institutions use a variety of the components (for a partial listing of Jones's client institutions, see the drop-down window list at *e*-education.com).

Launched on the Internet in 1995, JIU became the world's first purely on-line accredited university in 1999. JIU develops and offers courses, certificate programs, and degree programs to individuals worldwide, using a comprehensive array of technologies to increase opportunities, decrease costs, and provide an engaging and adaptable learning experience. JIU combines technology with educational content to deliver high-quality, convenient, affordable education. It has a rigorous instruction design process with the goal of optimizing use of the Web to maximize learning objectives and content. Technologies used include forums, chat rooms, streaming audio and video, and other Internet technologies to facilitate interaction among faculty members and fellow students.

Approximately 90 percent of JIU students are working adults who have computers in their homes or workplaces. Courses begin every four weeks and are scheduled in both eight- and sixteen-week terms. This enables students to fit coursework into their own schedules. Students receive many of the instructors' lectures and course notes via the course's Web site, and they spend most of their on-line time in chat, or discussion, groups with the instructor and other students. Though assignments, quizzes, and final exams are required on certain dates, students can withdraw or take a leave from their coursework because of work or family commitments. Course extensions can be arranged if necessary. There is little interruption in the continuity of each course because a student can go on-line, complete assignments, and participate in class discussion on a more flexible schedule than is the case with traditional classrooms.

Registered students receive a schedule of their courses each semester. In addition, an on-line catalog indicates what dates a course will be offered and gives a description of its content, credit hours, and cost. As the Internet's capability integrates more broadband infrastructure, starting semesters, terms, or courses weekly, daily, or even hourly may become feasible. Hypothetically, under this system a student could register for a course and begin the coursework an hour after enrolling. Such an arrangement would be designed to be student-centered; the student's time would determine when the course begins and at what time participation takes place.

Because the extent to which the Web-delivery software modules are used varies among JonesKnowledge.com's client institutions, the following discussion of how an individual student can take a course uses JIU as the example. The majority of the features and services described also would be found at a client university's or corporation's course-delivery Web site.

GETTING STARTED

Students who sign up for courses at JIU have access to JIU's Student Handbook, available in a PDF file at the Web site; it also can be viewed directly via a browser. The purpose of this material is to streamline the administrative process as much as possible so that the student's efforts go into studying and learning rather than into filling out forms and standing in lines.

This on-line handbook explains administrative procedures, grades, transcripts, and other relevant information such as enrollment and transcripts, withdrawal deadlines; it also provides instructions on how to drop a course, a schedule of tuition and fees, and information on the on-line *e*-global Library, the Knowledge Store (an on-line bookstore), and career services. An assignment matrix, syllabus, or e-mail from the instructor outlining course details and covering information such as assignments and exams is also available on the course's Web site. If the course calls for a proctored exam, this information also will be included.

ORIENTATION

An on-line orientation familiarizes JIU students with the university, its services, and course-related technology. The orientation has two main objectives: teaching students how JIU courses are structured and how to use the discussion software feature, course Web pages, and overall course technologies. All students are required to participate in the JIU orientation prior to the start date of each course to answer their questions and update them on JIU policies and procedures.

ATTENDANCE

Once the preliminaries are taken care of, students are ready to start participating in class, in their homes or offices. This sounds unstructured; however, the relative luxury of off-campus learning does not absolve students of good personal study habits. Although the courses are instructor-led, considerable responsibility is placed on the student for managing time for course participation and completion of assignments. Most JIU students stress the importance of managing of their personal schedules to maintain course continuity and to stay on top of assignments.

SUPPORT

When students have questions about scheduling, classwork, or related concerns, JonesKnowledge.com representatives at the Education Center will work with them to help resolve course completion problems. Essentially, the center takes the place of on-campus services for both the student and the affiliate university. In regard to the use of *e*-education software, the center, and other services of the company, JIU is viewed and treated on the same basis as other clients.

The center is staffed at JonesKnowledge.com's headquarters in Englewood, Colorado, USA. It supports the JonesKnowledge.com-affiliated colleges and universities and the administrative needs of participating students. Through the center, the company's representatives assist students with enrollment, bill them for tuition and fees, mail textbooks and support materials, and arrange exams. Center staff also refer students to local schools when appropriate and provide information about transfer of credits. Instructor contact is maintained via telephone, mail, e-mail, and periodic teleconferences to review course topics.

Table 6: Cost of One Year at a University			
Institution	Tuition	Books	Total
Harvard	$21,342	$650	$21,992
Jones International University	$ 3,750	$625	$ 4,375*

Source: *The New York Times Magazine,* 1999   *Graduate-level tuition cost

PAYING FOR A JONESKNOWLEDGE.COM EDUCATION

JIU is a good example of how public/private partnerships can bring together the best of both worlds for the benefit of the consumer — in this case, the education consumer. Students can do coursework at JIU for much less than the cost of the same on-campus experience at a private institution (Tables 6 and 7). Tuition costs at JIU fall midway between those of most public and moderately priced private colleges and universities. But JIU students pay only for their education — not for school-related transportation, housing, athletic or health fees, or other costs incurred in living away from home — plus they can keep their jobs.

Beyond the financial savings is the conservation of something equally as precious: time. Though the rigors required for success in a course are the same, JIU students don't have to spend time away from their jobs or families as students who attend classes on campus do.

THE NEED

The need for public/private partnerships such as JonesKnowledge.com, JIU, and participating institutions has never been greater.

Traditional university campuses, public or private, operating in a traditional way, cannot accommodate the educational needs of the expanding number of people who need and want it. They don't have the facilities, and they don't have the money. And, I would argue, they might not have the entrepreneurial spirit needed to create and implement innovative solutions to educational delivery problems. These solutions should be addressed immediately, and they should be addressed by traditional educational institutions and entrepreneurial private-sector organizations in concert.

Here are some statistics to ponder:

- There are 5 million to 7 million part-time higher education students in the United States alone.

- From 1978 to 1993, the number of 25- to 64-year-olds attending U.S. schools rose 45 percent.[2]

Table 7: Four-Year Colleges 1999–2000 Estimated Costs Per Semester for Undergraduate (12 Credits)			
Costs	Public	Private	JonesKnowledge.com
Tuition and fees	$1,679	$ 7,690	$1,700
Room and board	2,365	2,980	Existing costs at home
Books and supplies	341	350	$459*
Transportation	329	279	Existing costs at home
Other	742	527	Existing costs at home
Total	$5,455	$11,826	$2,159 (plus costs at home)

Source: The College Board, New York, N.Y.; JonesKnowledge.com
*Includes required course software

- One year's tuition at an elite private university or college in the United States costs about $25,000.[3]

- According to the American Society of Training and Development, 65 percent of all jobs in the United States and most other developed countries in 2000 require some training or education beyond high school.

- UNESCO, the United Nations Educational, Scientific and Cultural Organization, estimated that by 2000 there could be as many as 1 billion illiterate people in the world. That number has increased by more than 100 million in eight years.[4]

- More than 100 million students across the globe drop out of school prematurely.[5]

- In China alone some 80 million potential college students await space in the country's filled-to-capacity university and adult learning system.

Beyond the statistics lies the disturbing trend that most of the world's knowledge is the preserve of the most highly developed countries. Disseminating that knowledge worldwide is imperative if we want a world where peace is the norm rather than the exception, where business and industry can find the workforce to create economic prosperity, and where individuals can have the opportunity to participate in that prosperity.

In addition, the teacher shortage discussed in Chapter 2 is not limited to the United States. UNESCO has estimated that more than

50 million teachers are needed worldwide at all educational levels. Payment for their services represents 50 percent to 80 percent of current public educational expenditures in almost all countries.[6] Adding courses delivered via satellite and cable TV or the Internet to a school's or company's offerings can provide some economies of scale. A conventional course, requiring a teacher and a classroom, incurs start-up costs each time it is taught. It is also limited in size. A distance course, once developed and produced, can be distributed at minimal cost to hundreds of thousands of students. Distance education is very cost-effective.

THE PRIMARY AND SECONDARY SCHOOL DILEMMA

In the United States alone, shifting economic and demographic patterns have left small, rural, and inner-city primary and secondary schools without the resources to teach students the variety of curriculums they need to succeed. JonesKnowledge.com initially attempted to reach those schools with special secondary school curriculums through a cooperative agreement with the TI-In Network, a Texas-based provider of live, interactive television instruction.[7] The attempt was unsuccessful, however, for a number of reasons. In particular, a certification requirement that courses delivered by video must be delivered in real time, across time zones, and corresponding to myriad class bell schedules proved extremely difficult to fulfill. Working with local bureaucracies proved daunting as well.

As I've noted, the U.S. Department of Education's Star Schools Program has succeeded in providing real-time video and on-line learning for primary and secondary schools in the United States. It's a program to watch closely. As JonesKnowledge.com and its affiliates are doing in higher education, Star Schools is helping to document and shape the role of technology and telecommunications in primary and secondary schools.

WHAT'S NEXT?

What's next for JonesKnowledge.com? Depending on the most current data available in 2000, there are either 900 million[8] or 1 billion[9] television sets in the world. More than 500 million personal computers are in use, and that number is expected to rival TV ownership early in the 21st century. Convergent devices, such as Web TV, will bring Internet services very quickly to much of the world. JonesKnowledge.com will continue to extend its reach. Through electronic platforms, we can direct our product, courseware from the world's universities, to virtually anyone, anywhere.

JonesKnowledge.com's approach to higher education will continue to be one of augmentation, not replacement, of existing educational institutions. JonesKnowledge.com firmly embraces the academic environment and extends it. Universities have different structures. Those structures haven't changed much for hundreds of years. We've simply introduced a paradigm shift in the delivery of higher education.

With respect to technology, what's next — in fact what's now — is the cable modem, fiber-optic links to homes and businesses, and satellite delivery of Internet along with TV transmissions. As direct broadcast satellite and other wireless delivery systems evolve and cable systems and lines are upgraded, high-speed modems will transmit the complex graphic images that currently take so long to download onto your home computer. This technology provides speeds 100 to 1,000 times faster than most modems connected to telephone lines, if the user is willing to pay; the exact speed is determined by the amount of traffic traveling the Internet at the time the material is being downloaded. High-speed cable modems work by means of the same combination of fiber-optic and coaxi-al cables that allow cable television subscribers to view the com-mercial programming accessible via cable. Theoretically, a cable modem can pump data into homes or offices at rates of nearly 10 million bits per second. When you use a cable modem to link to the Internet, the Internet becomes like television; just point and click, and you're there.

Cable modems currently are expensive, but, as the technology is refined and the marketplace works its magic, prices will likely decline dramatically. Meanwhile, new telephone conglomerates are rapidly laying fiber-optic cable, and ADSL (asymmetrical digital sub-scriber line) technology allows the transmission of Internet content over old twisted-pair copper telephone lines at very high speeds.

As has been the case so far, it appears that the United States and Western Europe, including the United Kingdom, will be the first to benefit fully from these new and retrofitted technologies. However, satellite transmissions are allowing many developing countries to use cellular devices and leap-frog conventional wiring (in some cases, they must, because scavengers often tear out copper lines and sell them for scrap as quickly as they are installed). Other developing countries are simply accelerating their infrastructure upgrade. In early 2000, China's telecom companies were rushing to complete fiber-optic links among and within several major Chinese cities. Inexpensive Internet service was expected to follow quickly. Mary Modahl, Massachusetts-based Forrester Research Inc.'s group director, says our global fascination with technology makes us like "the Borg," the characters introduced on *Star Trek: The Next Generation,* who are half machine, half human.[10]

The telecommunications industry is looking toward a more competitive marketplace as the 21st century unfolds. Government regulators worldwide increasingly are opening their telecommunications infrastructures to accommodate competition. The benchmark, in fact, already has been set in the United Kingdom.

In the 1980s the U.K. government decided to allow competition in its telecommunications marketplace. As a result, enlightened government policy there has allowed and encouraged broadband operators — entities like cable companies — to deliver telephony and video products and services. Once these systems are completed, the United Kingdom will have the most elaborate, ubiquitously available electronic platform in existence. The rest of the world will have to compete with it.[11]

The United States followed suit with its Telecommunications Act of 1996. Though this legislation was originally touted as a competition-enhancing deregulation move, it actually led to substantial consolidation of that industry among major players in the United States. Nevertheless, the easing of regulatory restraints has improved the extent of telecom access and competitive pricing. Other countries are in the process of selling government-owned telephone companies to private-sector telephone service providers.

As competition takes hold in the world telecommunications marketplace, costs are expected to decrease and consumers will benefit. This has happened in the United Kingdom and the United States, and if the trend continues, it will ultimately happen around the world. This can only bode well for on-line education providers and students.

---

[1] Robert L. Hilliard, *Television and Adult Education* (Cambridge, Mass.: Schenkman Books, Inc., 1985), 122.

[2] Gene Koretz, "The Boom in Adult Education," *Business Week*, 10 July 1995, 24.

[3] John Elson, "The Campus of the Future," *Time*, 13 April 1992, 54.

[4] Jacques Delors, "Education for Tomorrow," *The UNESCO Courier* (April 1996), 9.

[5] Asher Deleon, "Learning to be: in retrospect," *The UNESCO Courier* (April 1996), 11.

[6] Robert Bisaillon, "Schools at the Crossroads," *The UNESCO Courier* (April 1996), 26.

[7] As the use of telecourses and other video-based programs has increased, so too have the number and type of groups providing programming alternatives. Some, like Pacific Mountain Network, function as a clearing-house of information and programs for a network of member educational institutions. Others, such as Canada-based TV Ontario, produce their own high-quality programs and sell them to educational institutions around the world.

Several of the largest providers are nonprofit consortia comprising member states, educational agencies, and educational television authorities. Two highly successful examples of this type of programming provider are the twelve-state Satellite Telecommunications Educational Programming Network, based in Washington state, and the nineteen-state Satellite Educational Resources Consortium, headquartered in Columbia, S.C. Both have received Star Schools Program funding from the federal government.

Commercial program providers have stepped forward to offer other programming alternatives. These alternatives are useful as supplements to in-class instruction but typically do not carry secondary school or university credit. For example, cable television operators have joined together to provide schools with newscasts from Cable News Network, as well as current events and other informative programming from such channels as C-SPAN, Discovery, Arts & Entertainment, and Disney. The cable industry has coordinated much of its efforts under the name Cable in the Classroom. Its offerings to date are without commercials and exclude, incredibly, most for-credit distance education. JonesKnowledge.com has contributed its *e*-global Library to this effort. Under Cable's High Speed Education Connection, the industry also has committed to provide free high-speed Internet access to elementary and secondary schools across the United States.

[8]"TV Viewing Soars Globally," *The Futurist* (September–October 1995).

[9]Parker Rossman, *The Emerging Worldwide Electronic University: Knowledge Age Global Higher Education* (Westport, Conn.: Greenwood Press, 1992), 139.

[10]Harvey Blume, "Touchstone," *Wired*, May 1996, 127.

[11]Recognition must be given here for the contributions of Jon Davey, Director of Cable and Satellite at the Independent Television Commission in the United Kingdom, one of the world's most visionary, even-handed, perceptive, and respected regulators. The United Kingdom's regulatory scheme, as of this writing, remains an outstanding world model.

With the development of the Internet, and with the increasing pervasiveness of communication between networked computers, we are in the middle of the most transforming technological event since the capture of fire.

> —John Perry Barlow,
> in *Harper's Magazine*

THE INTERNET COMES TO SCHOOL

In the mid-1990s, arguments raged among faculty, school administrators, and Internet proponents about whether the Internet should be a formal part of education's infrastructure. For those who resolved the argument in favor of the Net, another formidable barrier had to be confronted: where would the money come from to provide technology access in cash-strapped schools and university systems around the world?

Then an amazing phenomenon took hold. Students of all ages began bringing the Internet to school in the form of Web-delivered research and the results of e-mail chats with their peers about their assignments. At the same time, both private industry and governments began designating contributions and budgets to provide Internet access and more computers for classrooms. This coincided with a decrease in the cost of Internet hardware as the price of computing chips dropped to an all-time low. By late 1998, the price of an individual computer workstation dropped to less than a thousand dollars, down from two to three thousand only a few months before.

Innovative computer uses on the part of students, along with industry and government initiatives and the economics of inexpensive micro-computing, launched an enormous thrust forward that completely overwhelmed the Internet's detractors within the educational establishment. In a process characterized by its near-perfect symmetry, a technology born in the research labs of major government and university research institutions was opened to vast consumer markets and then flowed back into education through a multipronged approach that made it far more valuable.

Between 1996 and 1999, the number of U.S. K–12 schools with Internet access increased from 32 percent to more than 90 percent. In early 2000, connectivity in classrooms moved ahead in other countries as well.

THE WEB IS MAINSTREAM

At the end of 1994, *Business Week* touted the World Wide Web as "the hippest, most exciting neighborhood on the Internet." In the 21st century, the Web is beyond hip; it's mainstream. Somewhere in the graphics of nearly every television commercial or promotional announcement, there's a Web address. Even if they aren't "wired," most people in North America, Europe, many parts of Asia and South America, and some parts of Africa know that www.something.com or .org is an Internet Web address.

In a true testament to the Internet's cultural acceptance, Hollywood immortalized it on celluloid in the 1995 film *The Net,* and that was barely the beginning. From futuristic high-tech thrillers such as *The Matrix* and *Independence Day* (in which computer viruses were fed to alien invaders) to traditional romantic comedies such as *You've Got Mail,* the wired world has been adopted by the celluloid camp. If not the new darlings of entertainment, at the very least the Internet and computers are ready-made plot devices that no gimmick-minded screenwriter or director can pass up.

Louis Platt, president and CEO of Hewlett-Packard, calls the Internet the newest utility, right up there with water, power, and telephone service. In fact, the Internet is converging with the utility industry as gas and electric companies string fiber-optic lines through gas pipelines and send bits and bytes along high-transmission electricity lines. Andrew Laursen, vice-president of network computing at Oracle Corporation, says, "The Internet will subsume television, radio, and retail. The Internet will be everything."[1]

In distance education, the Internet truly is a transforming technology. Hudson Institute scholars Chester Finn and Bruno Manno contend that "even if we have only the PC and the Internet, we have enough to revolutionize education."[2] Through electronic delivery, it is possible to shift the emphasis in education from the institution to the student, where it belongs. And it is possible to deliver education more cheaply. As I've mentioned, it is becoming more apparent every day that fiscal concerns will shape education, its quality, and how it is delivered.

We now have the ability to organize information and manage it like we've never been able to before. And we have a critical need to lower the cost of education. We must strengthen educational institutions — it's in everyone's interest — and at the same time realize that the notion of educational institutions as physical places — real estate, if you will — is diminishing. Everyone in higher education will be affected by the Internet, including college presidents, regents, and faculty members. The Internet allows smaller classes and more one-on-one interaction with students, via electronic chat rooms and e-mail. Finn and Manno envision an on-line educational resource in which course lectures are available not in 50-minute chunks but in two- to five-minute video segments closely matched with a paragraph of the textbook and a video of an expensive-to-duplicate demonstration, with problem sets right at hand.[3]

THE FUTURE IS HERE

Manno and Finn's vision is already a functional reality. Currently, many distance learning certificate and degree programs offer courses via the Internet and World Wide Web that use combinations of video streaming, e-mail, on-line chat groups, and text-based materials. There is a book devoted entirely to cataloguing Internet-based higher education worldwide,[4] and a quick browse through the Web reveals on-line public and private university offerings galore. Transformed from a concept that was considered esoteric and a hard sell in the mid-1990s, on-line course offerings are now almost commonplace, though the quality of many reflects what is generally available in the traditional academic world.

Programs that are accredited attract most of the students, but on-line diploma mills proliferate and prey upon the impatient and unwary. Although hundreds of traditional universities now offer individual courses and a few full degree programs on-line, only one purely "virtual" institution had been accredited as of this writing (see Chapter 5).

In the United States and Canada, dozens of schools offer on-line courses. A visit to the web site www.geteducated.com provides a current, if not complete, sampling of the many on-line degree programs, including 20 undergraduate, 36 graduate, and 21 training and personal growth programs offered in the United States and Canada.

Among the offerings listed there are bachelor's and master's degrees in:

- distance learning from Athabasca University, Canada's Open University;

- engineering and business administration from Auburn University;

- education and human development/educational technology and leadership from George Washington University;

- engineering from Georgia Institute of Technology;

- business administration and business communications from Jones International University;

- media studies from the New School University;

- business and technology, information systems, and engineering management from New Jersey Institute of Technology;

- adult education plus certificates in business logistics, geographic information systems, and educational technology integration from Pennsylvania State University; and

- liberal arts studies from Skidmore College.

Web sites listing bachelor's degree programs, degree completion programs (usually for students who have completed two or more years of college coursework), and numerous certificate and personal skill programs now proliferate. The biggest challenge for the student is gauging which ones are of high quality and affordable.

Through Pennsylvania State University's virtual classroom, students can take courses such as the popular on-campus "History of Sexuality," "Grant Writing Tips for Health Care Professionals," and "A Nurse's Guide to the Internet." Long a leader in distance education, Penn State has used e-mail in its independent study courses since early 1995 and now fully uses Web delivery. Indiana University offers its journalism students electronic field trips to the Cable News Network center in Atlanta, Georgia. They also can access journalism periodicals from all over the world.[5]

ON-LINE PIONEERS

An on-line pioneer, the University of Phoenix (www.phoenix.edu) offers both undergraduate and graduate degree courses in cyberspace. All are business- and technology-related. Entrance requirements are similar to those of traditional on-site universities, but with a few additions. For example, for undergraduate admission, an on-line student must have a high school diploma or the equivalent, be at least 23 years old, and have had at least two years of post-high-school work experience with exposure to organizational systems and management processes. In addition, students must already have earned 24 credit hours from some other higher education institution. For graduate work, the requirements are equally rigorous. Class size is limited to 13. (No distance learning class should have more than 25 students per tutor or instructor, according to distance education expert Paul Levinson, head of ConnectEd.[6])

Terri Hedegaard, vice-president of on-line programs at the University of Phoenix, says the school's on-line effort has been successful. After several years of operation, "We think we're there," she says. "For us it began as an outreach method. We picked the [on-line] medium because it's very supportive of the adult teaching/learning process. It's interactive, which is the way adults learn."

WORLDWIDE LEARNING REVOLUTION

The on-line learning revolution is not confined to the United States. As early as 1993, British Open University (BOU) was contemplating expanding its services by creating an electronic campus. It followed through with these aspirations in late 1998 and 1999 when it opened a sister campus program in the United States. BOU's U.S. facilities are in Delaware and Colorado.

In Latin America and other developing areas of the world, on-line and other electronic educational options arguably are the most cost-effective way to educate enough of the population to bring those countries into the 21st century knowledge age. Inflation and interest on huge foreign debts have had a profound impact on educational funding in Latin America. Thirty-five years ago Latin American countries were able to send their best and brightest abroad, mostly to the United States, for graduate studies, but it is now "prohibitively expensive" to do so.[7] Likewise, building new bricks-and-mortar campuses doesn't seem to be a viable option. In addition, universities in Latin America often can't afford increasingly expensive scholarly journals.

Some of the groundwork for distance education in that part of the world already has been laid. Costa Rica and Venezuela, for example, have distance education institutions: Universidad Estatal a Distancia in Costa Rica and Universidad Nacional Abierta in Venezuela. In addition, the Monterrey, Mexico, Institute of Technology (ITESM, www.mty.itesm.mx) beams television courses complemented by Internet resources via satellite to 26 locations in Mexico and to others throughout North and South America. The courses are taught in Spanish and English.

Additional new offerings on the Internet are announced regularly in Europe, South Africa, Brazil, Argentina, Asia, Australia, and New Zealand.

LIVENING UP K–12 EDUCATION

With apologies to all the world's hard-working teachers, for kindergarten through 12th grade, on-line education is beginning to put new life into curriculums.

Consider the Global Schoolhouse (www.gsn.org). It's an internationally recognized K–12 project funded through a public/private partnership that includes the National Science Foundation, Cornell University, the University of Illinois, AT&T, Cisco, Farallon, Sprint, SuperMac, and Zenith Electronics. Students in 12 U.S. states and six other countries share information on cooperative projects. They use e-mail, the World Wide Web, and live video teleconferencing with their PCs. Projects they've worked on include alternative energy sources, solid-waste management, space exploration, and weather and natural disasters.[8]

The Global Schoolhouse is the brainchild of Global School Net Foundation, a 501(c)(3) nonprofit corporation, which wants to be known as a major contributor to the "philosophy, design, culture, and content of educational networking on the Internet and in the classroom," according to the Global Schoolhouse home page on the World Wide Web. From its beginnings in the mid-1980s when it was founded by schoolteachers in San Diego, California, with no budget and minimal support, Global School Net has emerged as an internationally recognized piece of the global education infrastructure.

Then there's KIDLINK (www.kidlink.net), founded by Odd de Presno, a Norwegian journalist and author of computer books.

KIDLINK is sort of a global kids' coffeeklatch, where kids from classrooms all over the world can discuss topics, through the KID-FORUM, such as "Environment 2093," "Native Literature," and "Cost of Living."[9]

In Florida, Space Coast Middle School in Port St. John is completely wired. The school opened in August 1995 with 1,650 sixth-, seventh-, and eighth-graders. It was designed as a model technology school for the Brevard County, Florida, school district. All 80 classrooms are wired for Internet access; 300 Apple Macintoshes grace the classrooms.

In Maryland, the Montgomery County public schools have instituted a Global Access plan to electronically connect classrooms, media centers, and offices so students and staff can access information and communicate locally through an "Intranet," computers with software tools and access to networked resources in each school's media center. Full implementation of the Montgomery County plan was expected to take six years and cost $70 million.

In California, NetDay '96 was created and sponsored by Sun Microsystems to get 12,000 Golden State public and private schools wired for access to the Internet on March 9, 1996, using volunteers from the business community. NetDay '96 wired, to some extent, about 30 percent of the state's schools all in one day. It was so successful that North Carolina and nearly 20 other states in the United States followed suit with their own Net days.

The U.S. cable industry has been wiring classrooms since 1989 through its Alliance for Education initiative. Some 8,400 cable systems and 32 national cable networks have wired 75 percent of U.S. public and private K–12 classrooms. These classrooms receive free 525 hours of educational television, specifically designed for the classroom, every month.

Cable companies also are creating wide-area fiber-optic networks connecting community educational resources in rural and urban U.S. locations. For example, in Mercer County, New Jersey, Comcast Corp. and a 14-member local educational consortium created MercerNet. This network links all Mercer County school districts, Mercer Community College, and a local science center with one another and with each of the county's public libraries and state colleges.

The network provides interactive TV for distance learning and community programs, high-speed cable access to the Internet, and high-speed data connectivity via cable, interfaced with multimedia video libraries in and out of the United States. With help from a $700,000 grant from the National Telecommunications and Information Administration, 14 interactive video classrooms with multiple-data channels were connected to MercerNet. Similar projects are under way in South Dakota, Louisiana, Michigan, Kentucky, Virginia, and California.

ON-LINE LEARNING IN CANADA

Canada, long known as a leader in distance education because of its far-flung population, has Internet-delivered and -complemented courses in secondary schools throughout its provinces. For example, British Columbia's CONNECT and OSCAR (Open School Courses and Resources), use Internet tools to teach subjects through K–12 schools in the province. These programs are available under the direction of the Open Learning Agency of British Columbia. Similar offerings are available in the other provinces.

CONNECT (web.desconnect.com) is operated jointly by nine distance education schools in British Columbia and delivers a variety of courses. This program offers flexible scheduling, electronically delivered courses, and continuous mediation and support for K–12 students at home, in learning centers, independent schools, and secondary schools. Course support includes special projects, alternative units, course adaptations, and various resources posted on-line. Some courses use multimedia CD-ROM resources, and others may be completed on-line. Students have e-mail links to their instructors and peers and may participate in on-line discussion groups or teleconferences with outside experts.

OSCAR (www.openschool.bc.ca/oscar) is directed to the high school, or upper school, curriculum and offers 14 on-line courses necessary to meet British Columbia's graduation requirements. OSCAR courses for grades 11 and 12 are delivered seamlessly to a school in on-line or print formats. OSCAR is for students in regular, distance education, or home school programs. Many courses require additional resources such as textbooks, software, and source guides. These courses are available to any school anywhere, providing the school has the right Internet connectivity and an instructor available to deliver the in-person portion of the course.

THE QUESTION OF ACCESS

The effort to get primary and secondary school classrooms in the United States wired is commendable. But are enough potential distance learners able to use the Internet or other on-line systems, not just in North America, but worldwide?

There's good news and bad news on this subject. The statistics on Internet usage are impressive. In 1985, for example, there were only 300,000 registered e-mail users worldwide. In 1993, there were 12 million people who used e-mail and other on-line services just in the United States.[10] In 2000, the figure in the United States was some 134 million users. In 1976, only 50,000 computers existed in the entire world. In early 1996, more than 50,000 computers were sold worldwide every 10 hours.[11] In 2000, the United States and Hong Kong had the highest computer-per-person ratios in the world, at one for approximately every two people. Canada's ratio was not far behind, at one for every four Canadians, and Australia's was slightly higher. The United Kingdom also boasted one computer for every four of its citizens.[12]

Among the developed nations, and in some of the fast-progressing lesser-developed countries such as China and India, both computer ownership and Internet connectivity are increasing at a pace that has outstripped even the most optimistic forecasts of the mid-1990s. This is due to the rapidly decreasing cost of basic PCs — down from $3,000 in the mid-1990s to less than $1,000 in early 2000 — and to the rapid demise of trade barriers to electronic imports and deregulation of the telecommunication industries.

In late 1995 and early 1996, Internet connectivity for schools in the United States still seemed a distant goal. At the end of 1995, only 35 percent of U.S. public schools had access to the Internet; only 3 percent had any individual classrooms connected.[13] But a dramatic change was about to occur.

The nation's economic boom and rapid deployment of technology gravitated into the public education sector more quickly than most experts assumed it could. In a feat of technology adaptation and market penetration whose only likely parallel is the production and deployment of military arms in the United States during World War II, most of the nation's 86,700 public schools were wired in a little over three years.

In the United States at the end of 1999, 90 percent of K–12 public schools reported they had Internet access, and 71 percent had access in at least one classroom, demonstrating that the technology had extended beyond school libraries and computer labs.[14]

Much of this progress was made possible by grants and assistance from U.S. companies in the computer and technology industries. A large part of the task was also funded by public and government investment channeled through normal appropriations.

Still, the schools that did not have Internet access were a concern, giving rise to claims of a "digital divide" between those with adequate computer and on-line access and those without it. Those without were primarily poor inner-city school districts and some of their rural counterparts.

A 1996 article in *Newsweek* magazine illustrated this circumstance all too clearly. The story was about a California-based high-tech chip-maker, MIPS, that wanted to help rural and inner-city schools gain access to the Internet. MIPS gave more than $55,000 to a school in Brooklyn, New York. The school didn't use it to buy computers. "They had a more urgent need," the article reported. The school administrators used the money to buy desks and chairs.[15]

The story pointed out some glaring inequities in U.S. schools, but make no mistake — the trend toward using the latest telecommunications technology in teaching either on site or at a distance and at every level is no passing fad. Cost of technology is no longer considered a barrier, at least in the developed world, though lack of teacher and administrator computer literacy is a continuing concern.

INTERNATIONAL CONNECTIVITY RAMPS UP

A disturbing statistic is often tossed into conversations about technology by telecommunications analysts: only half the world's population has ever made a telephone call.

In its 1999 Human Development Report, the United Nations devoted a chapter to "new technologies and the global race for knowledge." The primary point of the authors is that countries that are members of the Organization for Economic Cooperation and Development (OECD) must focus on making technology access equitable at all levels of global society. But the report's second level of impact is more graphic. Many of the trends and comparisons cited in the report give startling credence to the breakneck character of the globe's rush toward adaptation and convergence of computer, Internet, and other telecommunications technologies and other scientific breakthroughs. Any way you choose to look at it, nothing quite like it has happened before. For example,

- It took 38 years for radio to achieve 50 million users worldwide; it took the World Wide Web four years.

- Software exports from India rose in value from zero in 1980 to $1.5 billion U.S. in 1997.

- Sweden and the United States each have more than 60 phone lines per 100 people; Argentina and Saudi Arabia each have more than 10 lines per 100 people; Haiti, Kenya, Sierra Leone, Bangladesh, Tanzania, Uganda, and Afghanistan each have less than one line per 100 people.

- Thailand has more cellular phones than all of Africa.

- English is used in almost 80 percent of Web sites, including the graphics and instructions, even though fewer than one in ten people worldwide speak English.

- Industrial countries hold 97 percent of all patents worldwide.

- Use of intellectual property rights is alien to many developing countries.

- The United States has more computers than the rest of the world combined.

- Building telecommunications infrastructure does not ensure people will have the skills to use it.

That last point brings us back to the focus of this book, education and new ways to deliver it. The same United Nations report outlines a growing trend to provide the technology, training, and educational services necessary for people to convert their learning into employable skills.

In terms of grassroots initiatives toward cyber education worldwide, the report cites several examples:

> Building people's capacity to use the Internet starts in schools. The Costa Rican government has installed computers in rural schools across the country to give all pupils a chance to learn the new skills. In Hungary the ambitious Sulinet (Schoolnet) has enabled students in more than two-thirds of secondary schools to browse the Net from their classrooms. The annual NetDay initiative in the United States has used volunteers to connect more than 140,000 schools at a fraction of the commercial cost. Beyond classroom connections, support staff are essential for on-line learning, and teachers need training. In Finland teachers receive more than a month of training in how to use information technology in the classroom. In Lesotho the Technical Enhanced Leaning Institutes in Southern Africa (TELISA) were launched in 1998 to renew regional education with professional development for teachers.[16]

Still, there is much to be done. Despite the widespread, rapid deployment of computers and the Internet, at the dawn of the new millennium, less than 3 percent of the world's population was connected to the Net.[17]

What's Next?

Is there something out there in the ether that will revolution-ize distance learning beyond the new horizons of the Internet and the World Wide Web? Perhaps something simpler, faster, cheaper than laying phone lines and buying desktop PCs will make even faster growth possible, upping the 3 percent connectivity to 20, 30, or even 50 percent.

For starters, there are increasingly affordable personal com-puting/Internet access terminals; some are even available for free in exchange for the user signing up for several years of Internet access. Satellite delivery of Internet services can also speed up the accessibility of Internet service providers (ISPs) in rural areas and developing countries.

The proliferation of cellular phones in such countries as India, China, Mongolia, Russia, and various archipelagoes such as Indo-nesia has accelerated affordable telecommunications access in these countries by at least a generation ahead of most predictions in the early 1990s. One trend that has driven increased access has been the deregulation of telecommunications markets. In country after country, from Germany and the United Kingdom to Singapore and Hong Kong, as telecommunications access has been opened to private, market-based ownership, the price for consumer serv-ice has fallen. Now it looks as though access to computing power may enjoy a similar leap forward.

Greater bandwidth is coming as quickly as companies can install it, undersea cables can be laid, and satellites can be launched. Utility companies are mutating into true "utility" providers — and becoming telcommunications and cable TV competitors — by stringing fiber-optic lines through natural gas pipes, laying new cables along utility rights-of-way, and sending telecommunications voice and data over high-power transmission lines. They are also acting as telecommunications brokers, redirecting traffic along available infrastructure according to demands and user bids, just the way electricity is distributed over continental grid systems.

The gigapop. Another link in the greater bandwidth revolution is the gigapop. A pop is a point of presence, or the connection of a network to the Internet. A gigapop is a supersized pop, which allows information to move at a rate of 1,000 megabits per second, some 100 times faster than the speed of a typical university computer network and 4,000 times faster than the speed of a typical household modem. Gigapops are already being employed on campus systems and are greatly speeding the delivery of information — and classroom options — from professors to computer-equipped lecture halls. A student who is at home and who has the option of switching to a cable modem or other high-speed connection can also benefit from the wider, faster bandwidth. The Seattle Community College installed a gigapop in 1999 at a cost of $10,000, plus contributions of reduced service prices from local TV stations and a partnership with the University of Washington.[18]

Internet 2. Already operational, Internet 2 is the product of more than 100 U.S. research universities that banded together in 1996 to build a better, faster Net that would be their own. This is a very different Net from the consumer-access Internet. Internet 2 uses a hybrid mix of university, government, National Science Foundation (NSF), and other existing communication networks plus an array of new network tools not commonly used in the primary Internet — sort of a son of Superman who performs his miracles only for .edu sites.

The universities plan to hold on to Internet 2, and its design is not intended, or necessarily appropriate, for commercial and consumer use. Internet 2 makes maximum use of such complementary technology as the gigapop.[19] It also addresses the speed of response needed for individual transmissions and the problem of connection interruptions, something that the current Internet can't mitigate or solve. Although the universities don't intend this to be a new electronic backbone for everyone, they do intend to develop and prove new technologies that will make an eventual Super Internet for everyone much superior to what is available today.

VBNS. Another big bandwidth development that will benefit education in particular is VBNS. Begun in 1995 — just as NSF was turning over Internet 1, its brainchild, to commercial operators — VBNS is the product of a cooperative agreement between NSF and MCI. It is a noncommercial research platform for the advancement and development of high-speed applications and data-routing and data-switching capabilities. It also serves as an initial interconnect for Internet 2 members.[20]

With greater bandwidth, classrooms and individual students will soon be able to download and interact with video streaming technology — essentially, interactive TV over the Internet. The difference is that this can occur in real time. Every student can have a microcamera, and classroom interaction — as well as remote lab and field trip investigations — will no longer be restricted by time and place.

Video streaming technology. This technology has been available since the mid-1990s, and in 2000 college faculty and K–12 teachers were scrambling to acquire the skills to use it, just as they had to develop Web skills in the last four years of the 20th century. For some, the adaptation of video streaming will intensify the debate over the "edutainment" of education; for others, it will be seen as a tool that can convey both instructor and student into real-world environments that previously could only be described, read about, or viewed secondhand.

How about "smart card" technology? A smart card looks like your garden-variety credit card, but it's capable of tracking and organizing a distance education student's learning programs with the same degree of efficiency and pervasiveness as credit cards track individual finances.[21]

As the personal communication system (PCS) replaces the telephone, allowing everyone in the world to have the same phone number for his or her entire life, smart cards will become the way individuals access and interact with all manner of information, experts predict. For example, let's say you are on vacation in Germany and need to check up on an assignment for which you've forgotten the due date. Attached to your PCS is a smart card with a microelectronic circuit that keeps track of, among other things, your educational progress. Slip it into a smart card "reader" or perhaps a computer terminal, and it will display the current status of all your coursework.

According to Barry Barlow, an educational technology expert at the University of Saskatchewan, smart card technology will be interactive. Most of the work on smart card technology is being done in Europe.

What about virtual reality? Virtual reality is "a complete environment" assembled and managed by a computer software program. Instead of manipulating two-dimensional images while sitting at a keyboard, the virtual reality participant dons a special interface — right now a pair of goggles — that allows him or her to become part of a three-dimensional program.[22] For example, ScienceSpace, an evolving "suite of virtual worlds" that helps students master difficult science concepts, has been created by Chris Dede and his colleagues at the Graduate School of Education at George Mason University in Virginia.[23] Dede says virtual reality is more like diving into an aquarium as opposed to looking at fish through the aquarium's window.

Three virtual worlds currently are in various stages of development at George Mason:

- NewtonWorld allows students to dive into the world of one-dimensional motion;

- MaxwellWorld puts students inside electrostatics; and

- PaulingWorld allows students to experience molecular structure from the inside out.

By becoming part of the phenomenon, virtual learners gain "direct experiential intuitions about how the natural world works," Dede contends.

Then there is the Remote Exploratoriums project at the University of Colorado, Boulder. Using a programming environment called Agentsheets, Remote Exploratoriums are designed to take students who are navigating the World Wide Web beyond the passive role of viewing to the active role of building artifacts. Learning environments already developed include a simulation world for electric circuits, a model of melting ice, and a virtual ocean ecological system.[24]

The new technology is out there. It's all possible. What makes sense for distance educators to use remains to be determined. It is hoped the technology that can provide the greatest access to education for the greatest number will be at the top of distance educators' shopping lists worldwide.

[1]Nikhil Hutheesing, "Web Snarl," *Forbes*, 8 April 1996, 100.

[2]Chester E. Finn and Bruno Manno, "What's Wrong With the American University?" *Wilson Quarterly*, 20 (winter 1996), 48.

[3]Ibid.

[4]Dan Corrigan, *The Internet University: College Courses by Computer* (Harwich, Mass.: Cape Software Press, 1996).

[5]Eric C. Richardson, "Internet Cum Laude," *Internet World*, October 1995, 41.

[6]Parker Rossman, *The Emerging Worldwide Electronic University: Knowledge Age Global Higher Education* (Westport, Conn.: Greenwood Press, 1992), 10.

[7]Rossman, *Worldwide Electronic University*, xiii.

[8]John R. Vacca, "CU on the Net," *Internet World*, October 1995, 81.

[9]G. Davies and B. Samways, eds., "KIDLINK, Creating the Global Village" *Teleteaching*, (North-Holland: Elsevier Science Publishers, B.V., 1993), 837.

[10]Emilio Gonzalez, *"Connecting the Nation: Classrooms, Libraries and Health Care Organizations in the Knowledge Age"* (U.S. Department of Commerce, 1995), 4.

[11]Ibid.

[12]Jeffrey Young, "I.Q. Wars," *Forbes ASAP*, 4 December 1995, 78.

[13]Gonzalez, *Connecting the Nation*, 10.

[14]Pamela Mendels, "Internet Access Spreads to More Classrooms, Survey Finds," *The New York Times*, 1 December 1999, Technology Section, www.nytimes.com/library.

[15]David A. Kaplan and Adam Rogers, "The Silicon Classroom," *Newsweek*, April 1996, 60.

[16]Human Development Report 1999, United Nations, New York, 65.

[17]Ibid, 62.

[18]Dale Carnevale, "Professors take distance learning to next-generation networks," *The Chronicle of Higher Education*, 11 November 1999, A60.

[19]Royal Van Horn, "Internet 2 and InternetE. ," *Phi Delta Kappan*, January 1998, 413.

[20]Ibid.

[21]Barry Willis, ed., *Distance Education: Strategies and Tools* (Englewood Cliffs, N.J.: Educational Technology Publications, Inc., 1994), 32.

[22]Ibid, 226.

[23]Chris Dede, "Emerging Technologies and Learning," *American Journal of Distributed Distance Education,* 1996, 10(2), 4–36.

[24]Ibid.

**The open society, the unrestricted
access to knowledge, the unplanned and
uninhibited association of men for its
furtherance — these are what may make
a vast, complex, ever growing, ever
changing, ever more specialized and
expert technological world, nevertheless
a world of human community.**

— J. Robert Oppenheimer,
in *Science and the
Common Understanding*

DISTANCE LEARNING: DEFINING THE MARKET

Where there is a need, there usually is a market. Distance education is no exception.

The global market for distance education delivery is burgeoning, be it via satellite and cable to television sets or via telephone line and the Internet to computers. Estimates are that distance learning in the United States alone is a $1 billion industry in 2000. That is an increase of more than 100 percent since 1992–93. Worldwide, the distance education market is estimated at $9 billion.[1] When we look at the developing world's need for education, we see that these estimates are just the tip of the iceberg.

Of the 6 billion people now on the globe, 1 billion are teenagers,[2] and this demographic group will likely continue to grow in developing countries for at least the first half of the 21st century. To a great extent, the amount of education available to them will determine the success of their countries' economic development.

In the United States, the number of students needing traditional higher education has been predicted to climb from 15 million in

111

2000 to 20 million by 2010.[3] "Traditional" in this case means post-high-school programs at an accredited two- or four-year institution or programs and courses that are accredited through such institutions. That's a 30 percent increase in demand in barely a decade. Perhaps this doesn't sound too daunting in a time of relative economic prosperity, until we are confronted with the fact that there were only 15 million postsecondary classroom seats in the United States at the beginning of 2000. Paradoxically, institutions were having great difficulty funding building programs and recruiting faculty to serve students who often were only able to attend part-time. Add to the projected student body another 90 million U.S. adults who want part-time continuing education beyond the traditional two- and four-year programs, and we see a considerable bottleneck. This, in addition to the sudden availability of affordable technology, may explain why traditional U.S. institutions developed more distance learning capabilities between 1995 and 2000 than they did during the entire previous half-century.

CHINA'S EDUCATION MARKET

Other solutions are being applied or devised in other countries, depending on the technology available. China's higher education infrastructure illustrates my point. The higher education system in China counts about 2,000 universities, colleges, and adult education institutions that enroll 4.5 million to 5 million full-time and part-time students in both bachelor's degree and nondegree programs. In 1998, 2.52 million students graduated from China's college-preparatory-level senior general secondary schools.

Because of space and intense competition, only 1.2 million were admitted into higher education institutions.[4]

Another 4 million students who graduated from non-college-prep programs at secondary schools were potential candidates for additional training. Attempting a rough estimate of potential adult learners in China, whose population at last count was 1.3 billion, brings the total potential distance learners in just that one Asian country exponentially higher. A devout believer in distance education, China has one of the biggest distance learning programs in the world through the China Central Radio and Television University, with more than 1.5 million students taking the courses offered over radio and TV. As more computers find their way into China's homes, the technology will undoubtedly shift to Internet delivery.

There are challenges, to be sure, in delivering electronically based higher education to different parts of the world. In Japan and Korea, delivering higher education on the Internet is not a problem, although overcoming the language barrier presented by English-based education is a hurdle. In India, where expertise and technological savvy are in place and where English is either the first or second language for many people, the caste system creates barriers for many potential distance learners.

The issue for Asia — with the exception of India and a few other countries — is that the culture of learning is different. It is, by and large, one way, from teacher to student, and is based more on memorization than is U.S.-style higher education. It is necessary to keep this in mind in developing distance education courses that bridge

Western and Asian cultures.

In the rest of English-speaking East Asia — Singapore, Malaysia, parts of Indonesia, Hong Kong, and the Philippines — there is an enormous demand for higher education. The telecommunications infrastructure has been developed quickly, making distance education feasible in the metropolitan areas. Australia and New Zealand are long-time leaders in distance education. The market in both countries is both wired and proven.

EUROPE'S DEMAND AND CHALLENGES

There is demand in Europe, although the potential student population is smaller. British Open University provides the potential for higher education at a distance to nontraditional students from all over the European Union.[5]

In Europe, the challenges facing distance education are cultural, not technical. Especially in western Europe, computers are increasingly part of the furnishings in the homes of most of the intelligentsia and middle class. Satellite technology is advanced all over Europe. As in the United States, TV is everywhere. But Europe in general does not have a tradition of promoting open access to education, despite the great success of British Open University.

The market also is substantial in South America and Africa. Although these populations are large and growing, telecommunications and cable infrastructure is less ubiquitous. It will take some time for the technology to become widespread. When it does, however, these markets will boom.

In Africa, the challenges are political, social, and economic. In the mostly Muslim north, there is a small group that can afford to tap into technology-delivered distance learning. But, in general, the masses of people in that region don't have access.

In central Africa, the same factors are at work, but to an even greater extent. Only one country in the region can be considered even moderately stable: Kenya. And the percentage of the population that can afford more than the most basic standard of living is minuscule.

In South Africa, the situation is better. At least 25 percent of the country is ready to receive technology-delivered distance education. It's interesting to note, however, that South Africa has had television only since the mid-1980s.

For generations, South Africa's black and colored population was provided with less than adequate education under the policies of apartheid. Now, the South African government hopes to remedy the public education deficit using distance education technology. But first things first. Many rural areas and townships have yet to receive electricity.

Africa is getting some help on the technology-based distance education front from at least one international organization, however. The World Bank is working on a project to create a virtual university that would cover the entire continent.

In North America, the United States and Canada are wired, and the market for distance education is huge and proven. In Mexico, the Monterrey Institute of Technology is leading the way with satellite-delivered and Internet-augmented distance education. Mexican professors also have their own listserv on the Internet, called Profmex. Even though there is the cultural barrier of an entrenched class system in Mexico, the last three elected governments in that country have voiced a commitment to universal education.

In Central America and South America, politics, culture, and technology access are the challenges. Central America, which includes the Caribbean, has a significant English-speaking population, but politics are turbulent, and universal access to technology is a distant goal. In South America, with the exception of Chile, the same challenges apply, and the languages are Spanish and Portuguese. In addition, faculty unions in universities are entrenched and powerful. Although many faculty members are exploring electronic platform delivery, many others do not welcome technology-based distance education.

Despite these hurdles, however, I believe information highway technology will be available in most parts of this vast planet sooner than most people think. Among others taking this optimistic view is A.W. Bates, executive director for research and strategic planning at the Open Learning Agency in British Columbia, Canada. In 1993 Bates predicted that within the next 10 years the integration of computers, television, and telecommunications through both digitization and compression techniques would become commonplace.

Bates also predicted the costs for such integrated systems would go down, and they have, drastically. In March 1996, U.S.

computer maker Gateway 2000 introduced Destination, a combination TV-computer for the home market.[6] The new machine used a Pentium chip–based personal computer with special accessory cards for high-quality sound and video and was attached to a 31-inch computer monitor. It included a wireless keyboard and a remote control. At the time Destination was launched, its suggested retail price was $3,800. Since then, WebTV, which was quickly purchased by Microsoft, entered the market with a set-top box and keyboard that provide the basic hardware needed to connect most TVs to the Internet for $200. According to several industry analysts, this is only the first of what is expected to be a flood of convergent technology and big-screen home computer/video systems that will effectively place classrooms, laboratories, and professors' offices in the living rooms of the world.[7]

A CAMPUS FOR EVERY CONTINENT

In 1966 the most advanced transatlantic telephone cable could carry only 138 simultaneous conversations between Europe and North America. In 1988, the first fiber-optic cable carried 40,000 simultaneous conversations. The fiber-optic cables of the 1990s carried nearly 1.5 million.[8]

In 2000, with satellite technology it was possible to beam distance learning programs to every continent of the world. A global electronic campus using existing telecommunications satellites and fiber-optic cable is possible. The campus's reach would encompass the satellites' footprints on Earth (Figure 6), and much of the content could be delivered by the global Internet.

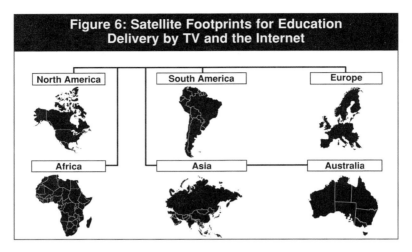

Figure 6: Satellite Footprints for Education Delivery by TV and the Internet

North America | South America | Europe

Africa | Asia | Australia

The infrastructure to pick up satellite signals is multiplying. In the subcontinent of India alone, the number of cable TV–equipped homes receiving satellite channels almost doubled between 1993 and 1994, from 7.5 million to 14 million. By 2000, India expected to have 80 million cable TV–equipped homes able to receive up to 250 digitally compressed services.[9]

With the availability of cheap computers, India in particular is rapidly becoming a global center for computing services. It has the opportunity to be a leader in distance education applications.

WORLDWIDE ELECTRONIC CORPORATE EDUCATION AND TRAINING

Higher education delivered electronically worldwide is not just constrained to the kind that culminates in a university degree. It also is appropriate for executive education and training. In that realm, the educational delivery pendulum is swinging toward technology at an ever-increasing rate. Corporations, now lean and mean, can't afford the luxury of sending managers to one- or two-week training programs off site. Indeed, *Business Week* magazine quoted one U.S. CEO as saying, "If we can do without someone for a week, we can probably do without them for good."[10]

Though less than 20 percent of training was delivered by technology in 1995, *Corporate University Xchange*, an industry newsletter, forecasted that by 2000 more than 50 percent would be delivered by some mix of videotapes, audio tapes, CD-ROMS, interactive video conferencing, satellite-delivered training, and training on the Internet.[11] U.S. corporations alone spent about $30 billion on executive education and training, roughly 1.4 percent of their payrolls. This percentage jumped to 2.5 percent if the U.S. corporation was among the Fortune 500.[12] In Japan and Germany, the portion of an employee's time dedicated to education and training runs between 8 percent and 10 percent.

WHO'S DELIVERING DISTANCE CORPORATE EDUCATION?

Universities, nonprofit organizations, and public/private partnerships are beginning to beam corporate education and training almost everywhere. The delivery modes vary from real-time, video-based instruction to Internet-based virtual training programs.[13]

Here are a few examples:

National Technological University. A leading work-site-delivered electronic corporate education program is National Technological University (NTU), based in Fort Collins, Colorado. Since 1984, NTU has offered courses and graduate degree programs to engineers via satellite. NTU is a consortium of university departments of engineering. It is run as a private, nonprofit corporation and is governed by a board of trustees, most of whom represent industry.

Faculty are located on their respective university campuses, and students take courses at their work sites. Classes are available on the Internet or are televised on multiple channels 24 hours a day, seven days a week. Most courses are recorded at the students' work sites for use at their convenience.

NTU students use e-mail, fax, telephone, and conventional mail to interact with instructors. They are able to take advantage of the combined expertise of engineering faculty at 48 participating universities, including Arizona State, Alabama, California, Colorado, Maryland, Michigan, Minnesota, Columbia, Cornell, Purdue, and Rensselaer Polytechnic Institute. NTU is financed through student tuition.

In early 1996, NTU began offering its degree programs internationally via satellite. Twenty universities in Thailand, the International Medical College and Motorola in Malaysia, a university in Indonesia, several locations in Australia, and Motorola in Korea received NTU's courses. NTU's satellite delivery footprint covers the entire Pacific Rim.

The biggest challenge for NTU's international expansion has been language. In Malaysia and Australia, where English is spoken, there is no problem. But in Thailand, NTU courses will probably have to be "language-mediated" for the foreseeable future.

Europace. NTU was the model for a similar consortium of universities in Europe called Europace. It serves business and technical professionals in European industry via satellite and the Internet, offering tele- and video conferencing as well as live conference events. As of mid-2000, the organization listed 45 universities as member organizations, plus 15 industry and government organizations. Europace's satellite footprint covers 18 countries in which there are 329,000 educational institutions and a population of potential learners of about 44 million.

Ford Motor Company. Many corporations create their own electronically based "corporate universities" to deliver education and training worldwide. Ford Motor Company, for example, created its own satellite-delivered closed-circuit television network, FordStar, the largest privately owned satellite network in the world, according to Ford. It was designed and developed specifically to deliver training and information programming to Ford dealerships in North America and, ultimately, around the world.

The network has more than 2,000 receiving sites in North America. Ford uses similar satellite TV technology to deliver two training programs to 10 manufacturing sites in North America.

Ford also piloted an on-line management training course over its in-company Intranet. The course, on effective meeting planning and management, was targeted to 500 to 600 Ford employees.

For Ford, the driving force behind piloting the Intranet-based training program and other electronic platform-based distance education and training was the Ford 2000 initiative. Begun in 1995, Ford 2000's objective was to integrate company programs globally. The company no longer looked at itself as comprising separate units but as a whole organization with 300,000 employees who just happened to be located in different facilities around the world.

As a result, for Ford, distance education via electronic platforms was not a passing fad, said a supervisor in Ford's Education and Training design and development division.

"Our philosophy for the use of distance learning is that it is one platform of delivery in a family of options. We are looking at an integrated delivery strategy for learning, not an individual technology such as the Internet, video, or CD-ROM. We want to incorporate all of [these technologies] into the process," the supervisor said.

JonesKnowledge.com. Jones also delivers corporate education and training, both through Jones International University and via the company's *e*-education™ software clients.

Courses can be delivered through a combination of satellite, video, and Internet-based technologies. Manager-students communicate via e-mail, Internet chat rooms, and voice mail. Course delivery isn't confined to real time, and customized equipment isn't necessary. As a result, the programming can be delivered to more than one location at a time.

Manager-students take management training courses, including master's- and MBA-level curriculum, at home or at work on their own schedules. Staff at Jones work with industry partners to develop degree and certificate programs.

In Barbados, Canada, and Antigua, and at Mercedes-Benz and Siemens A.G. in Germany, students also are taking MBA-level courses from the University of Colorado at Colorado Springs using *e*-education software and services.

U.S. Universities Tap the Market

Back in the world of degree-granting institutions, New York University is a good example of a provider of electronically based higher education and training. The university has created the Virtual College, which claims to be the first higher education interactive teleprogram to deliver interactive video to computers in students' homes. All course materials — video, simulations, laboratories, and readings — are digital and are accessible through a single common user interface.[14]

The Virtual College uses IBM's Lotus Notes groupware and a Lotus product called Video Notes. Students can log on anytime and communicate with classmates and instructors through an e-mail system. They also take exams and check grades on-line.

The college is not for everyone. It offers only courses that lend themselves to the use of technology. Mainly adult learners — mostly managers in mid-career — can earn an advanced professional

Certificate in Information Technology that is designed to prepare them for work with on-line information systems. NYU's Virtual College students have included employees from British Airways, Chemical Bank, ITT, NBC, NYNEX, and the United Nations.

Using different info-technology, the University of Michigan is offering a customized MBA degree via video conferencing to managers at Daewoo Corporation in Korea and Cathay Pacific Airways Ltd. in Hong Kong. Michigan's business school also is working with a consortium of companies to deliver courses via live video transmission and the Internet in the United States, Europe, and Asia.

THE GLOBAL COURSE PROTOTYPE

Creating the content for electronically delivered international courses is no easy task. Although worldwide use of the Internet is increasing at a dizzying pace (Table 8), cultural barriers in different areas of the world continue to make development of electronic coursework content a challenge.

Most courses are simply taught in the language and within the cultural framework of the country from which the course emanates. Others are modified for local audiences.

There are courses, however, that were designed from the outset for an international audience. One particular course comes to mind. In 1991, the Annenberg School of Communications and the Corporation for Public Broadcasting (CPB) joined forces to fund and distribute an electronically delivered course known in the

Table 8: Growth in Number of Internet Users by Country					
Country	**1997**	**2000**	**Country**	**1997**	**2000**
Australia	1.21 million	7 million	**Germany**	4 million	15.9 million
Canada	4.6 million	13.3 million	**India**	80,000	4.5 million
China	200,000	16.9 million	**Japan**	8 million	27 million
Finland	500,000	2.15 million	**U.K.**	960,000	19.4 million
France	400,000	9 million	**U.S.**	45 million	134 million

Source: Nua surveys, www.nua.ie

United States as "Inside the Global Economy."[15] A group of educators and public television broadcasters from several countries met and collaborated on the video-based course. Besides the Annenberg/CPB group, the TELEAC Foundation of The Netherlands, the Swedish Educational Broadcasting organization, JL Productions of Chile, and the Australian Broadcasting Corporation were partners in the effort.

A 13-lesson video course was the outcome. Each lesson is based on an examination of two case studies. In addition to the 13 one-hour videos, the course requires a textbook in international economics, a course reader — created as a study guide for the course — and a software-based tutor that includes a glossary of terms, graphical analysis of data, interactive testing, forecasting simulations, and a databank of test questions keyed to the textbook chapters.

The course took three years to develop, was filmed in 20 countries, and was edited to fit the needs of each region in which it was shown. As this undertaking illustrates, creating content for a world-wide audience is not a simple task. But experiments such as "Inside the Global Economy" can teach us much.

The Internet takes this kind of curriculum one step further. Because of the World Wide Web's immediacy, using the Internet to deliver courses such as "Inside the Global Economy" enables content to be constantly updated, reflecting ever-changing world economic conditions.

THE ROAD AHEAD

The road ahead for electronically based international corporate education and training is still a bit bumpy, but it is definitely paved with a mix of satellite technology, silicon, and fiber. It is a road that corporations will travel. As I've noted, they have no choice. In a shrinking world, where global competition is truly inescapable and where market economies rule, businesses world-wide must keep each one of their workers — whether on the line or in the executive suite — current with cutting-edge management and technical training.

Businesses can do it themselves, they can contract with universities, they can contract with consortiums, or they can get involved in customized educational development partnerships. But they must train. They must educate. They must do it whether their employees are in Chicago or Calcutta. The key to success is finding the most cost-effective, flexible way to do it.

[1]The U.S. market is estimated to be 5 percent of the world total, but is also the most technology-enabled. In the absence of research data that compile all distance education markets on the same basis, $9 billion was derived by increasing the U.S. market estimate by a factor of 10.

[2]Samuel L. Dunn, "The Virtualizing of Education," *The Futurist*, March–April 2000, 34.

[3]Ibid.

[4]*Essential Statistics of Education in China*, 1999, www.moe.edu.cn/statics/p1.htm.

[5]G. Davies and B. Samways, eds., *Teleteaching* (North-Holland: Elsevier Science Publishers B.V., 1993), 1.

[6]Evan Ramstad, Associated Press, "Product Merges PC, TV," (Boulder, Colo.) *Daily Camera*, 24 March 1996, 1B.

[7]Ibid.

[8]Author unknown, "Magic Carpet Ride," *Cable and Satellite Europe*, 15 June 1995.

[9]Ibid.

[10]John A. Byrne, "Virtual B-Schools," *Business Week*, 23 October 1995, 65.

[11]Author unknown, "Corporate Universities in the Year 2000," *Corporate University Xchange*, January–February 1996, 3.

[12]Jeanne C. Meister, *Corporate Quality Universities: Lessons in Building a World-Class Work Force* (Burr Ridge, Ill., and New York: Irwin Professional Publishing, 1994), 12.

[13]Ibid.

[14]Author unknown, "NYU's Virtual College Delivers Distance Learning On Demand," *Corporate University Xchange*, March–April 1996, 6.

[15]Peter J. Dirr, "Media Review," *American Journal of Distance Education*, 9, No. 3, 1995, 85.

Some people are willing to push the envelope of education delivery. And, when they do, accreditation agencies will be there to validate all or part of it.

— Jack Allen,
    Southern Association of
    Schools and Colleges,
    Decatur, Georgia

THE ACCREDITATION DEBATE

In an electronic environment in which education, entertainment, and news blend into a phenomenon called edutainment, distance education and new concepts such as cyberschools risk being characterized as something less than serious higher education.

Definitions of what is and isn't technology-based distance education can become murky to the uninitiated. Is electronically delivered distance education what you learn while watching The Discovery Channel, The History Channel, The Learning Channel, or most of what's offered on public television in the United States? Of course you learn, and often the programs are compelling and of high quality. In fact, some excellent edutainment television programming — the PBS series on the U.S. Civil War, for example — is used as part of U.S. high school and college curriculums.

But there is a critical distinction between providing electronically delivered edutainment and providing electronically delivered distance education. The distinction is that one is credentialed, and the other is not. One requires examination and provides certification to students, and the other doesn't.

Degree- and certificate-granting distance education programs are serious educational endeavors, equally as serious as those located on college campuses. Education accreditation agencies, particularly in the United States, are beginning to officially recognize the importance and legitimacy of these programs, as well as their need for quality control.

PRINCIPLES OF GOOD PRACTICE

In the United States, two higher education organizations have developed what are called principles of good practice in electronically delivered distance education. They are the Western Interstate Commission for Higher Education (WICHE), Boulder, Colorado, and the American Council on Education, Washington, D.C.

The 17 WICHE principles were three years in the making and are called the Principles of Good Practice for Electronically Offered Academic Degree and Certificate Programs. They are essential reading for students considering enrolling in distance education programs and for institutions interested in offering such programs. They stress the development of rigorous educational outcomes, completeness of programs, adequate and appropriate interaction between students and teaching faculty, appropriate support systems and training for both students and faculty, course and student evaluations, and the importance of students' access to learning resources. WICHE's Principles of Good Practice are given in Appendix A.

The American Council on Education's principles for distance learning go into greater detail, but generally consist of five over-arching concepts:

- That distance learning activities are designed to fit the specific context for learning;

- That distance learning opportunities are effectively supported for learners through fully accessible modes of delivery and resources;

- That distance learning initiatives must be backed by an organizational commitment to quality and effectiveness in all aspects of the teaching and learning environments;

- That distance education programs organize learning around demonstrable learning outcomes, assist the learner in achieving these outcomes, and assess learner progress by reference to these outcomes; and

- That the provider has a plan and infrastructure for using technology that supports its teaching or educational goals and activities.[1]

The American Council on Education's principles also appear in full in Appendix A.

The council suggests, and I concur, that its principles of good practice should be applied beyond higher education institutions. All those involved in the learning enterprise — including individual learners, institutions, corporations, labor unions, associations, and government agencies — will benefit from principles that provide guidance in producing high-quality education with outcomes that can be clearly assessed. Strengthening one sector will improve the effectiveness of the others and, in turn, address the learning needs of individuals and society as a whole, the council's task force said.[2]

Numerous U.S. higher education accreditation agencies have adopted WICHE's principles. They include the Northwest Association of Schools and Colleges in Seattle, Washington; the North Central Association of Colleges and Schools in Chicago, Illinois; and the Middle States Association of Colleges and Schools in Philadelphia, Pennsylvania. Expectations are that the American Council on Education's guidelines also will be embraced. Both will guide accreditors in the increasingly frequent task of determining the quality of electronically delivered education. As Dr. Margaret Kraus of the Northwest Association of Schools and Colleges says, "The guidelines will give us stars to look out for."

ACCREDITATION: WHO CONFERS IT?

Accreditation historically has been the way for students to determine whether the institution they attend maintains certain quality standards. In most countries, the central government accredits higher education institutions. In France, for example, the federal government is the accrediting agency. In the United Kingdom, the federal government essentially supervises accreditation. In Canada, the provinces are responsible.

In the United States, the accreditation system works differently. Its different structure may make it a potential vehicle for certifying quality in electronically delivered international distance education. A look at the history of U.S. higher education accreditation provides some evidence for this notion.

Education in the United States has never been the responsibility of the central government. It isn't even mentioned in the constitution of the country. What the 10th Amendment to the U.S. constitution does say, however, is that powers not explicitly given to the federal government or denied to the state governments are the province of the states. Because education is mentioned nowhere, by default it became the states' responsibility.

In the 18th and early 19th centuries, the states did almost nothing about educating their populations. Even though the first public school in the North American British colonies was created by local edict in Massachusetts in 1639, education primarily was the province of private institutions. It was delivered through an intricate web of private preparatory schools that prepared students for private universities. Because of its exclusive nature, education was reserved for the upper classes.

The situation changed as the country expanded to the West and its citizens became more mobile. At the end of the 18th century, in the Northwest Ordinance passed by Congress in 1787, the federal government encouraged the founding of universities on its frontier — in wild and untamed places like Michigan. And in the first half of the 19th century, public primary- and secondary-level schools proliferated as a result of decisions by states to fund them through state taxes.

Because the frontier universities had no private preparatory school system from which to garner students, they were faced with what can only be described as a recruiting problem. The dilemma was this: How could they convince public school students to continue their education at a university?

The solution was not long in coming from the University of Michigan through a program called the high school visitor plan. University faculty would visit public high schools in their state and examine both students and faculty to determine whether the school's students were "university material." The Michigan Plan caught on, and soon university faculties throughout the Midwest were visiting high schools.

The practice became so prevalent that by the early 1900s high schools were complaining they were being overrun by state university faculty. In mock desperation, the high schools suggested the process be turned around and that colleges and universities be the institutions examined. In fact, that is what happened.

During the first half of the 20th century a series of nongovernmental, mostly volunteer, peer-review regional higher education accreditation agencies came into prominence. Today there are six for higher education: the Middle States Association of Colleges and Schools, the New England Association of Schools and Colleges, the North Central Association of Colleges and Schools, the Northwest Association of Schools and Colleges, the Southern Association of Colleges and Schools, and the Western Association of Schools and Colleges.

WORLDWIDE QUALITY STANDARDS

Because U.S. higher education accrediting bodies are non-governmental, some of their officials believe the United States could become the center for accrediting higher education programs worldwide.

"We may lead the way because we are not government-affiliated. That offers an edge to the United States. We can maneuver across international boundaries without competition. We also are able to transcend politics — if that's possible," contends Dr. Jack Allen, of the Southern Association of Colleges and Schools.

The Southern Association already accredits universities in Latin America. Among those with its stamp of approval are the Monterrey Institute of Technology — with multiple campuses in Mexico and satellite courses that can be beamed almost anywhere in North America — and the University of the Americas, with campuses in Puebla and Mexico City, Mexico. The University of Monterrey in Monterrey, Mexico, also is an applicant for Southern Association accreditation.

Global Alliance for Transnational Education. There is another international accreditation vehicle. It is affiliated with the

135

Jones organization and is called the Global Alliance for Transnational Education (GATE).

GATE was created in 1995 to develop quality assurance principles that can be used to evaluate electronically delivered education courses worldwide. The alliance's first conference was held in Denver, Colorado, in that year and was attended by educators from Canada, Chile, Hungary, Ireland, New Zealand, the People's Republic of China, South Africa, the United Kingdom, and the United States. Subsequent GATE conferences have been held in London, Paris, Melbourne, Washington, D.C., and Colorado Springs, Colorado.

As businesses increasingly draw their workforces from all over the globe, and as education and training are disseminated from its vast reaches, international measures of quality such as the ISO 9000 quality standard in international manufacturing are a necessity. Corporations and educators are just beginning to set the agenda.

Beyond setting principles for evaluating and certifying transnational education programs, the alliance is tackling ongoing projects that include amassing a database of higher education institutions throughout the world and developing an international quality assurance directory to help corporations and agencies evaluate the education credentials of potential employees. GATE's certification standards and process are explained in Appendix B.

WHAT ACCREDITORS THINK

Most accreditors in the United States believe the fundamental principles of quality they use to judge traditional education institutions apply to electronic distance education institutions as well. For example, the integrity of an institution's conduct in all its activities, honesty and accuracy, adequate financial resources to run programs, and the like are applicable to both traditional and distance education institutions.

But accreditors admit certain characteristics of distance education make it unique and present challenges for distance education institutions and accreditors alike. One challenge is to develop methods for determining whether students and faculty are sufficiently computer-literate to either instruct or successfully complete a Web-delivered course. How does the institution know, for example, if a student enrolling in an on-line degree program in business management is sufficiently knowledgeable in the technology used to deliver the courses to take exams?

One could argue that the same question might be asked at a traditional higher education institution about the ability of a traditional student to understand how to use the on-campus library. It's normally not an admissions requirement, but most students get the hang of it rapidly.

Other issues include student access to library resources and arrangements for students to complete curriculums that are dropped from electronic institutions. Many accreditation agencies require traditional universities and colleges to provide an independent study option or the option of completing the curriculum at another university. It would not be difficult for a cyberschool to do the same.

And what about institutional visits by accreditors? "How do you visit an individual computer?" the Southern Association's Jack Allen quipped.

These are not insurmountable issues. The key is for distance learning institutions, be they in the public or the private sector, to be aware of the requirements and provide for their fulfillment.

The North Central Association of Colleges and Schools (NCACS) perhaps has had the most experience dealing with the unique qualities of distance learning programs. Since the 1970s, it has accredited electronically delivered degree programs from National Technological University and distance learning programs delivered in part via electronic means from the University of Phoenix and The Union Institute (www.tui.edu). Union offers one of the few Ph.D.-granting distance learning programs in the world. And, as has been detailed elsewhere in this book, in 1999 and 2000, NCACS granted accreditations to Jones International University, first for its bachelor's and master's programs in business communication, then for its MBA program. Jones was the first purely virtual, completely on-the-Web university to receive full, normal accreditation from any of the recognized accrediting bodies in the United States.

Accreditation agency officials in the United States believe, as I do, that the trend toward technological delivery of higher education will continue. As Allen says, "I don't think there is any doubt about it, especially as technology gets cheap enough for everyone to have it in their home[s]. What happens is some people push the envelope of educational delivery. And when they do, accreditation associations will be there to validate part or all of it."

Pushing that envelope is the business of entrepreneurs. Those of us who are higher education entrepreneurs, whether from the private side or public side, are excited about the opportunity.

---

[1]Eugene Sullivan and T. Rocco, *Guiding Principles for Distance Learning in a Learning Society* (May 1996), 4.

[2]Ibid, 2.

It is the only solution for me at this point.

> — Igor Ciric,
> distance education student,
> formerly of Belgrade, Yugoslavia

CYBERSCHOOLS AND YOU

A HOW-TO GUIDE FOR DISTANCE LEARNERS

If you've decided that distance education is an option you would like to explore in furthering your education or training, there are several important facts to keep in mind as you look for courses of study that meet your needs.

DISTANCE EDUCATION, NOT INSTANT EDUCATION

First, distance education is not instant education. For the majority of for-credit courses delivered via technology, it is necessary to submit an application for admission to the program and arrange for academic records to be transferred from other educational institutions you have attended. After that, you must, of course, be admitted to the distance education course or program you have applied for. Even though many cyberschools will expedite this process, to gain admission to a distance education institution, you follow much the same process as you would to gain admission to a traditional institution. If you are applying to take courses via distance education at a traditional university — for

141

example, Pennsylvania State University in University Park, Pennsylvania, has a large distance education department — you must meet its admission standards.

A RIGOROUS WAY TO LEARN

Second, distance education is rigorous. Don't expect course-work to be easier simply because it is delivered via technology. Indeed, students must not only have the ability to absorb and understand the courses' content but also be disciplined self-starters. To an even greater extent than on a traditional college campus, no one will stand over your shoulder admonishing you to get your work done. It's up to you. And it should be. After all, you're the one getting the education.

DISTANCE EDUCATION, NOT PASSIVE EDUCATION

Third, when you are a cyberstudent, it's virtually impossible for you to be a passive learner. The approach to learning is active, not passive. In traditional classrooms, students can get by for weeks at a time sitting quietly taking notes — or not taking notes — and never actively participate in discussions with the instructor and other students. Many of us have done this at some point.

In a cyberschool, students nearly always must react or provide some appropriate input to continue to the next phase of an assignment. In addition, courses are more often designed to be collaborative efforts among students than are traditional lecture hall courses.

In some computerized courses, a significant part of a student's grade depends on participation in on-line discussion groups.

A Better Way to Learn?

Fourth, learning via technology may be a better way for some students to learn.

In its Apple Classrooms of Tomorrow project, Apple Computer, Inc., is investigating how teaching and learning change when people have constant access to state-of-the-art technology. The project began in 1985 and is ongoing. After the first 10 years, the project's conclusions were that students become re-energized and more excited about learning when using information technology. Grades improved, standardized test scores went up, and dropout and absenteeism rates decreased, according to Apple's report on "Teaching, Learning and Technology." As shown in Figure 7, the study reported that during the first 10 years of the project, dropout rates for participating high school students fell from 30 percent to zero.

Even before the Apple project's 10-year findings, it was reported time and again in research on how we learn at all educational levels that electronic instruction, either via teleconference or computer conference, can be as effective as traditional classroom-based lectures and face-to-face discussions. On-line students have test scores equal to those of students in conventional classrooms if the quality of the teaching is the same, they report better access to instructors, and they reportedly improved their ability to collaborate and communicate.

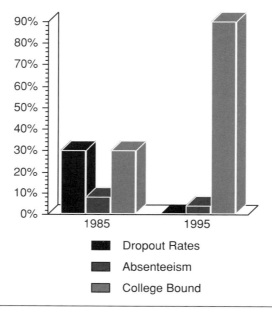

Figure 7: The Impact of Technology on Learning
·10-year results for high school students participating in
Apple Classrooms of Tomorrow project

Dropout Rates
Absenteeism
College Bound

Source: "Teaching, Learning and Technology," a report on 10 years of Apple Classrooms of Tomorrow Research, Apple Computer, Inc., Oct. 2, 1995.

TEN QUESTIONS TO ASK

Knowledge is power. It's a good idea to ask any distance education institution you are considering lots of questions. Here's a list of 10 to get you started.

1. **How technologically savvy do I need to be to take electronically delivered distance education courses?** It almost goes without saying that for distance learning courses delivered via technology, some degree of computer literacy is

necessary. Knowledge of the Internet, especially the World Wide Web and e-mail, is a plus.

That being said, there still are many distance education courses delivered via cable and satellite television. For those courses, knowing how to record classes from your television to a video-cassette loaded in a VCR often is necessary. It also is possible in many TV courses to purchase prerecorded videotapes of the classes. Today, however, many televised courses have an Internet component — even if that component is only using e-mail to communicate with your instructor or other classmates.

2. **What kind of information technology do I need to take these classes?** Usually a cyberschool will give you a list of the technologies that must be accessible to you when you apply for admission. Just in case a list isn't offered, you need to know whether you need access to:

- A computer — what kind and how powerful?
- A modem — what speed (how many bauds per second: 28,800? 56,000?);
- Any special software;
- An Internet connection;
- A television equipped with cable or satellite program delivery capabilities;
- A videocassette recorder/player.

Generally, you will need to have access to some of these tools. Special software, or courseware, is necessary for some distance education programs.

3. **What kind of student support structure does the institution offer?** Is there a way to contact someone about course advising, missed assignments, student emergencies, or any other question that might come up while you're taking courses at a distance? Is there a number to call? Is it an 800 number? Is there an e-mail address? What kind of library support services are available? Find out.

4. **Is the institution accredited?** This question is important for several reasons. First, and perhaps foremost if you are hoping to receive federal financial aid to attend classes at a cyberschool or at some less high-tech distance education institution, it's important to know that the U.S. government does not lend money to students attending nonaccredited institutions. Similar restrictions apply in other countries. In addition, though accreditation is not absolutely necessary for a school to stay in business and award certificates and degrees, a degree or certificate from an accredited institution is far and away more prestigious for a student. Primarily because they all are so new, many cyberschools are going through the accreditation process now, and their applications are being carefully scrutinized. According to accreditors in the United States, technologically delivered education is legitimate, and if it's not already recognized by a particular accrediting agency, it soon will be. For more information about accreditation, see Chapter 8.

5. **Will a degree I get from a cyberschool based in a country in which I'm not a citizen be recognized?** In the near

future, the answer to this question will more than likely be yes. Right now, among other international efforts, some cross-border accreditation is occurring between the United States and Mexico and the United States and Colombia. In addition, the Global Alliance for Transnational Education (GATE) is working on international distance education standards and an international education database. The database will contain information about universities and their programs around the world. For more information on GATE and cross-border accreditation, see Chapter 8.

Remember, for years students have gone to traditional universities in one country — for a bachelor's degree, for example — and with few if any problems continued their graduate education in universities in another country.

6. **Where do I buy the textbooks required for the course?** Textbooks still are part and parcel of any coursework. Make sure you know how and where to obtain yours.

7. **Are the instructors at the cyberschool trained to teach on-line?** This is a very important question to ask because teaching in cyberspace requires a different, more interactive approach than teaching students in a classroom.

8. **Is it possible to complete an entire degree program via technology through this institution?** To effectively plan your educational strategy, you need to know how much coursework you can complete on-line or via video.

9. **How long does it take to get a degree or certificate through this institution?** The answer may be the same amount of time it takes to complete a course of study at a traditional university, or it may be less. Often the timing is flexible, because one aspect of good distance education is that it allows the student to be in charge of the process. There also may be minimum and maximum allowable times. Check out your options.

10. **What if I start a degree program and find out when I'm in the middle of it that the program has been discontinued?** The majority of degree-granting institutions — whether they are cyberschools or traditional universities — make provisions for alternative ways to complete degree programs that have been dropped. Such provisions are required for an institution to be accredited. Find out what alternatives the institution in which you plan to enroll can offer you if it discontinues your degree program.

CYBERSTUDENT OPINIONS

In addition to asking questions, another excellent way to judge the quality of a cyberschool or other type of technology-delivered distance education institution is to listen to those who have gone through a program before you.

As I've mentioned throughout this book, students enrolled in distance education courses represent diverse backgrounds, a broad range of ages, and widely varied goals.

Many are striving to enhance their career opportunities or to attain other personal and professional objectives. Some audit courses simply out of curiosity or a commitment to lifelong learning. All cite distance teaching's focus on the student as a primary factor in their decision to take advantage of this nontraditional way to learn.

Following are several profiles of distance education students that might prove enlightening.

Though the profiles by no means represent the varied and plentiful distance learning programs available around the world, I hope they will help illustrate my point that the marriage between distance learning and information technology is living up to its promise as a way to make all the world a school, one that millions more can afford.

IGOR CIRIC
Toronto, Ontario, Canada, and Belgrade, Yugoslavia
Master's in Business Communication, Jones International University —
in progress

Igor Ciric is a mechanical engineer, originally from Belgrade, Yugoslavia. Ciric was studying on-line at Jones International University (JIU) for his master's degree in business communication. He already has finished courses in the fundamentals of business writing and basic public speaking.

His professional objective is not only to enhance his knowledge but also to add to his fields of expertise. Like many other distance education students, he also wants his educational credentials to lead to a successful business career.

He says his experiences with distance learning thus far are highly positive: "I have all the aids for learning at home and immediate assistance from professors by e-mail." The only difficulty Ciric sees with learning at a distance is the time it requires.

"I usually come [home] from work around 5:30 p.m., so I don't have much time left for all other activities. Studies need time and concentration, so sometimes days are pretty tough and it gets very hard to meet the deadlines for assignments."

Would he take courses via distance education again?

"Yes, I would. It is the only solution for me at this point."

REJANE LAMOUNIER FRANCA
Brookline, Massachusetts, and Belo Horizonte, Brazil
Certificate in Business Technology
Jones International University

Rejane Lamounier Franca is a marketing analyst for Audiolab Sistemas Eletronicos of Brazil. She was in the United States to scout opportunities for her company in the American marketplace, especially the software market. She is interested both personally and professionally in distance learning.

"Distance learning is a reality here [in the United States], and I have a great interest in seeing how it works. It's part of my business plan," Franca said.

She was working toward a certificate in Business Technology via distance education at JIU. She would be interested in getting a master's degree through JIU, but she's not sure whether she can get an Internet connection in her home country to continue her studies. If she can, she would take distance education courses again, she says.

Franca said her experience with distance learning was positive: "So far, so good. This is my first course, and I'm very impressed."

MANDY CAIRD
Denver, Colorado
Certificate of Course Completion, Virtual School of Natural Sciences
Globewide Network Academy

While working in medical research at a major U.S. university health sciences center, Mandy Caird discovered cyberschools. The neurology laboratory where she was a researcher received tremendous amounts of DNA-related data, and she needed more education to analyze the statistical significance of the data. "I wasn't necessarily looking for courses on-line," she said. But that's where she found one to suit her needs, in the Virtual School of Natural Sciences, run jointly by the Massachusetts Institute of Technology and Bielefeld University in Germany through the Globewide Network Academy (http://uu-gna.mit.edu:8001/uu-gna/index.html).

The course was taught completely via the Internet, in a virtual classroom with instructions given by e-mail. The 30 to 40 people enrolled were split into groups of six, and each group had its own Internet chat room.

"My teacher was in Mexico City," Caird said. Students were from Finland, Australia, and the United States. The course was taught in real time and used shareware.

Caird doesn't think the course was too high-tech for the computer-literate student. She did say, however, that the technological applications required to take the course made it more appropriate for those with powerful computers and Internet access.

PABLO LUCAS
Hollywood, Florida
Bachelor's in Business Administration, Regis University
Master's in Management Information Systems — in progress

Pablo Lucas began his higher education in the traditional way. A Florida resident, he first received an associate's degree from a community college in that state and then began working on a computer engineering degree at Florida International University (FIU).

He switched his major and his university when he discovered he could finish his bachelor's and get a master's degree through a distance education program in the time it would take him to graduate from FIU with only a bachelor's degree.

Lucas became Denver, Colorado–based Regis University's first graduate in one of the distance education degree programs it offers through JIU. He began a master's degree program in Management Information Systems in January 1996.

Lucas said distance learning provided him a better education than the traditional model, because, he believes, he learned more and retained more information. He appreciated the difficult, hands-on projects he was required to complete.

For Lucas, the best aspects of distance education are its flexibility and its cost. "My biggest concerns [about] returning to school were the time and money it requires. [Distance education] made these obstacles minimal issues."

LORRAINE PRIEST
Warren, Michigan
Master's in Business Administration, University of Phoenix On-line

Lorraine Priest is an information systems analyst at General Motors (GM). She has received all her academic degrees on-line, and she finished the final course for her MBA at the University of Phoenix's on-line campus.

She tried to go to college on the ground, but it didn't work. "It was too regimented. I couldn't raise a family and work and go to school," she said.

She rates her on-line collegiate experience as excellent.

For potential distance learning students who might not be cyberwise, Priest provides some advice and comfort. "All you need to know is how to turn on your [computer]. Nowadays most of the software is very intelligent, and there is always a person around to help you," she said.

Help from work and family is a plus. GM has a tuition assistance program that helped Priest with school expenses. And "my husband has done every bit of my laundry since I started school," she said.

When Priest completed her MBA, she planned to embark on an on-line Ph.D. program through the Fielding Institute (www. fielding.edu) in Santa Barbara, California.

The whole of science is nothing more than a refinement of everyday thinking.

— Albert Einstein,
in *Physics and Reality*

10

FREE MARKET FUSION: ONE PATH

The electronic delivery of education is an ideal prospect for a kind of public/private partnership I call Free Market Fusion, a management process I have studied for several years. It was chosen as the final topic for this book because it offers students, teachers, and public and private education planners a way of thinking about how they might find the resources to pursue electronic education.

My book, *Free Market Fusion: How Entrepreneurs and Nonprofits Create 21st Century Success* (Cyber Publishing Group, Inc., 1999), treats this subject in more depth and explores several case studies. A companion document, with interactive exercises, is available on the Web at www.freemarketfusion.com.

DEFINING FREE MARKET FUSION

What is Free Market Fusion? It is an entrepreneurial approach to identifying or creating opportunities for innovative solutions. In physics, fusion occurs when two elements combine to create a new element and, simultaneously, release a tremendous amount of energy. Rather than converting one form of energy into another, the reaction instead creates *new* energy. Fusion is one of the most powerful and energy-efficient processes known to the world; we race to find a means to safely harness its potential in the service of humanity.

Free Market Fusion is both a process and its result. It is a process that creates new products, services, and solutions and is typically based on new or modified concepts. Although portions of entire industries can be involved and permutations of participants can range widely, it is easiest to discuss the process by considering first a few examples that most clearly demonstrate the process and potential of Free Market Fusion.

Free Market Fusion is the coming together of two or more entities, one or more of which is characterized as a for-profit enterprise and one or more of which is characterized as an institutional, nonprofit, quasi-governmental, or governmental entity. For purposes of illustration, we'll call them *A entities* (for-profit) and *B entities* (institutional, nonprofit, etc.). The process typically culminates in the fusing of a portion, or possibly all, of the assets of one or more A entities with a portion, or possibly all, of the assets of one or more B entities. This relationship can be diagrammed as shown in Figure 8.

Although Free Market Fusion may result in the formation of new enterprises, typically at the outset, existing organizations are the creators. Also, typically the entities involved share a common need, concern, or opportunity that generates support for resolution. The collaborative process inherent in Free Market Fusion can engender the tremendous release of energies that comes from look-ing at the world not as a miasma of intractable problems but as an arena of challenges awaiting exploration, initiative, and solution.

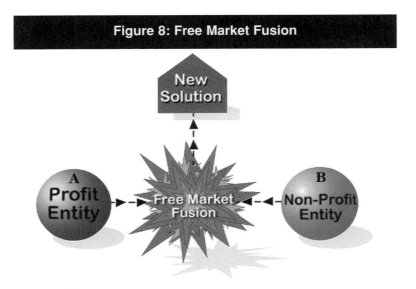

Figure 8: Free Market Fusion

WORKING TOGETHER

In the Free Market Fusion process, each entity contributes its particular strengths, agreed upon by both parties, to the project. For example, in a partnership between an entrepreneurial group and an institution, the entrepreneur might contribute the initial innovative idea as well as technological marketing expertise and significant risk assumption. The institution might contribute per-sonnel, physical facilities, familiarity with the existing market, and perhaps acceptability.

Depending on the parties, some of those roles might be reversed. However, the purpose of the partnership is always to enable both parties to accomplish goals neither could attain alone to create a solution where there was none. As in fusion, the new solution is accompanied by a breathtaking burst of energy as new possibilities and opportunities open up to everyone involved, both those creating the solution and those benefiting from it.

JonesKnowledge.com, discussed in Chapter 5, provides an example of the Free Market Fusion process. The entrepreneurial entity in this case was Jones International, a company initially involved in cable television and various other communications entities. The institutional partner was a selected group from the 3,400 colleges and universities that comprise the U.S. higher education community.

The problem (or opportunity) confronting higher education in the United States was that the size and nature of its constituency, workforce requirements, and educational costs were changing much faster than the institutions could respond. Enrollment of traditional students, fresh out of high school and committed to graduating from college within four years, was decreasing. Nontraditional students who were older, working, and often had family commitments were requesting alternative programs geared to their varied schedules and financial constraints.

The solution to this dilemma was to offer high-quality, college-level, for-credit courseware from colleges and universities across the country to students in their homes, offices, or libraries. In effect, it delivered education to the students rather than the students to education. This diminished the distance and time required to acquire education. And for students who could afford tuition but not the added expense of on-campus room and board and associated student costs, JonesKnowledge.com offered a way to make higher education financially accessible.

FREE MARKET FUSION, ENTREPRENEURS, AND INSTITUTIONS

A productive type of Free Market Fusion results from combining the strengths, resources, and assets of an institutional entity with those of an entrepreneurial group. In this situation, the strengths of the institution might include specialized subject knowledge, existing facilities, thorough understanding of a specific market, a strong administrative and management structure, and a history of solid, stable functioning.

The strengths and assets of the entrepreneur might include expertise in competitive strategies, the ability to evaluate risks and a willingness to undertake intelligent ones, commitment to innovative thinking, awareness of opportunities presented by recent technological advances, strategic networking abilities, an understanding of and familiarity with capitalization resources, and the ability to orchestrate the transformation of concepts into products.

The catalyst is leadership, which may or may not be provided by the freewheeling entrepreneur. The fact that an entrepreneur may be well known and accustomed to operating in the public spotlight does not mean that person will assume the leadership mantle or that he or she should.

Leadership encompasses much more than simply assuming the role of primary public spokesperson. The most critical leadership activities are intuition, imagination, planning, organizing, networking, and acting as missionary within the organizations involved, persuading and recruiting internal supporters for a new concept. Often individuals with established credibility within an institution can do this most effectively. The entrepreneur may assume some parts of this role or merely advise and be an "outside" networker, promoting the concept to other organizations and individuals whose support is essential. Even the process of leadership may be shared or fused. Entrepreneurs and institutions provide an especially effective example of Free Market Fusion because combining many of their core strengths enables them to accomplish what neither could accomplish alone.

INSTITUTIONS: INERTIA VERSUS INITIATIVE

Institutions are a critical part of society's infrastructure. They include schools, colleges and universities, hospitals, prisons, the military services, national charitable organizations, unions and professional organizations, quasi-governmental agencies, and such community entities as libraries, symphonies, museums, civic leagues, and innumerable religious groups. Often, they have existing physical facilities and a stable organizational structure. Successful institutions have a thorough understanding of their constituencies and of those constituencies' special needs and concerns. Often they bring the comfort of market acceptance because of their involvement in the new solution.

Institutions play an important role in reaffirming our sense of community, especially today when we are deluged with an onslaught of change on a regular basis. As connections to our past, they are familiar and comforting. Many of them have existed almost as long as the country itself; others grew with the needs of our growing nation. Harvard was established in 1636, Yale in 1701, and in 1862 the Morrill Act led to the establishment of the public higher education system. Today, the United States has some 3,400 institutions of higher learning.

The first lending libraries in the United States were founded by English clergyman Thomas Bray in Maryland in the late 1600s, and the country's public library system was launched nationally when Andrew Carnegie undertook funding the construction of 2,500 community library buildings between 1881 and 1891. Some 5,400 public libraries now are supported by communities across the United States.

The Boy Scout and Girl Scout programs, originating in Great Britain, were introduced in the United States in the first decade of the 20th century and now involve well over 7 million children, teens, and adults. The YMCA, with 25 million members in more than 90 countries, has been a pillar of thousands of communities since its inception in London in 1844. And U.S. towns and cities have relied on community hospitals ever since Philadelphia's Pennsylvania Hospital first received its charter in 1751 through the tireless efforts of Benjamin Franklin.

Institutions have played a central role in advancing the goals of society throughout history. It is imperative that they remain as vital and forward-thinking as possible if they are to continue their positive impact on society. This is no easy task; it is in the nature of institutions (and of monopolistic businesses) that stability may deteriorate to stagnation and management to mediocrity. Even Thomas Jefferson recognized this possibility, when he wrote:

> I am not an advocate for frequent change in laws or constitutions. But laws and institutions must go hand in hand with the progress of the human mind. As that becomes more developed, more enlightened, as new discoveries are made, new truths discovered and manners and opinions change, with the change of circumstances, institutions must advance also to keep pace with the times. We might as well require a man to wear still the coat which fitted him when a boy as civilized society to remain ever under the regimen of their barbarous ancestors.[1]

Over the past several decades, we as a society seem to have lost confidence in the ability of our institutions to perform with competence and integrity the functions for which they were created. As circumstances have changed, often institutions have failed to change with them, choosing instead to hold onto the more familiar, less-threatening solutions of yesterday and to be protected by the environment that depended on them.

The tendency of institutions and large organizations to rely on solutions drawn from yesterday's realities was pointed out some two decades ago by Peter Drucker in his article "Managing the Public Service Institution":

> No success lasts "forever." Yet it is even more difficult to abandon yesterday's success than it is to reappraise failure. Success breeds its own hubris. It creates emotional attachments, habits of thought and action, and, above all, false self-confidence. A success that has outlived its usefulness may, in the end, be more damaging than failure. Especially in a service institution, yesterday's success becomes "policy," "virtue," "conviction," if not indeed "Holy Writ," unless the institution imposes on itself the discipline of thinking through its mission, its objectives, and its priorities, and of building in feedback control from results over policies, priorities, and action.[2]

RISK-TAKING: THE KEY ROLE

A complementary relationship between entrepreneurs and partnering institutions relates to risk-taking. Missteps within an institutional environment can easily spell the end of a promising career, a circumstance that has an obvious (and understandable) dampening effect on an institutional leader's willingness to take risks. In addition to identifying opportunities, then, another of the entrepreneur's key roles in a Free Market Fusion venture is to assume a substantial amount of the risk involved in any new undertaking, thus diverting a large measure of the "exposure" from the institution's leader to the entrepreneur.

COMBINING RISK-TAKING AND CAUTION

This imposes no hardship, for although risk-taking is anathema to an institution, judicious and well-informed risk-taking is second nature to the entrepreneur. An entrepreneur has the freedom to respond to opportunity with a desire for gain rather than resisting it because of a fear of loss. Similarly, because entrepreneurs are not part of the "old guard" operating environment of the institution and have minimal vested interests in conforming to established ideologies, they are much freer to envision radical alternatives and innovative solutions outside the boundaries of accepted practices.

Thomas Jefferson believed that every generation needed its own revolution. In the United States, entrepreneurs have always been society's revolutionaries, playing from outside the boundaries, creating new solutions for a changing world. Now they have an opportunity to chart new ground once again.

Exploring this new frontier will take discipline and commitment to a common vision, because the gains to be won through society's revitalization will be more long-term than immediate. No work is more critical, however, for the well-being of the world; we simply cannot continue to exist, let alone compete fairly in the global marketplace, if major portions of our population or our infrastructure are left to perish in the wasteland of yesterday's solutions.

MODELING FREE MARKET FUSION

The major components of any Free Market Fusion process are:

1. Identifying and evaluating potential Free Market Fusion opportunities.

2. Creating an innovative solution.

3. Identifying potential partners.

4. Structuring the relationship.

5. Undertaking the project.

Obviously, every situation will demand different levels of time and energy at each phase. However, if participants know from the outset that there is a process to work through, then resources can be allocated accordingly.

If an innovative solution incorporates a fairly nontraditional concept, it will be easier to work with a partner who already is comfortable with the nontraditional concept. For example, in the late 1980s JonesKnowledge.com combined a nontraditional delivery process (cable television) with a nontraditional teaching method (telecourses). The colleges and universities that had not previously used telecourses were not nearly as likely to be comfortable with the concept represented by JonesKnowledge.com as were the schools that understood the potential of telecourses and had already integrated them effectively into their programs. The same applied to the use of Internet technology in the mid-1990s.

Another consideration is that many potential partners may be constrained by people or organizations whose vested interests might be threatened by the entity's move into a new arena or into a relationship with another (autonomous) entity in which the vested interests have no control. A major contributor to the organization, for example, may forbid it from entering into any new relationship for fear that the contributor will lose his or her tacit control of the organization's goals and direction.

This is a fairly predictable response. Fear of change is a familiar reaction, especially for constituencies, such as labor union memberships or government or large business entities, that fear they may lose previously protected positions. Therefore it becomes critical to strive for an acceptable level of friction, in which the fear of change is counterbalanced by enthusiastic commitment to the opportunity at hand. This control relationship may not surface initially, but when it does, it often terminates further negotiation.

STRUCTURING THE RELATIONSHIP

Once the concept of a Free Market Fusion venture is developed, then the manner in which these entities and their functions, equipment, personnel, or activities can be joined must be considered. What are the costs? Who must contribute what? Who might feel threatened? Who will manage the process? What kind of time frame will it take for Free Market Fusion to function? What are the risks involved and who will take them? What is the reward system? The list of potential questions to be answered is long and will vary with each project.

Obviously, each project will have its own set of circumstances and concerns that need to be addressed and agreed on before other steps can be taken. However, the following areas can serve as a starting point from which to explore and negotiate.

Goal issues. What are the purposes and goals of this project? How will achievement of the goals be measured? How and when will they be evaluated? What is the reward structure?

Inertia issues. Best-laid plans can easily be derailed by organizational inertia. How rapidly will both parties be able to respond to opportunities or crises? How rapidly are both parties *willing* to respond?

Structural and logistics issues. How will the project be undertaken? Where and how will it be located — centralized with one participant, headquartered at a project site? Who will implement what aspects of the project?

What is a reasonable and mutually agreeable time frame? This can become a key issue if both parties do not understand and accept how long it will take to accomplish key tasks. If the project will entail working with large institutions, government agencies, or other bureaucracies, (including bureaucratic businesses), the time from start to completion could be substantially extended.

Competition issues. How will you deal with competing players? Will you work around their established programs, trying not to disrupt their "market share," or will you try to displace their "product" with your own.

Much care must be taken in dealing with societal concerns. Society is rarely damaged when, in the rough- and-tumble competitive market of consumer goods, a candy bar or a laundry detergent or a sports car line bites the dust. However, when societal issues are addressed, often a less-than-terrific solution may be worth keeping because it provides ancillary benefits.

Long-term issues. Assuming the project is successful in meeting its goals and is profitable, what should become of it in the long term? Should the relationship between the participants continue as is, or should it be reviewed on a specified basis? Should the project continue in its current form or be taken over by one of the participants? Should it be taken public as an established company? Should it move into other Free Market Fusion arenas?

OPPORTUNITIES FOR FREE MARKET FUSION

There are many areas in which a Free Market Fusion approach currently is or soon will be enabling us to make more creative, effective use of the technological tools now available. A few examples follow.

Health Care. It has become clear over the past several years that the world's health care crisis is going to demand radical measures and innovative solutions. The twin goals of cost containment and universal access to basic levels of medical care will obviously remain mutually exclusive unless efficient, cost-effective alternatives can be developed and implemented rapidly. A Free Market Fusion process combining the strengths and knowledge of the medical establishment with the vision and technological savvy of entrepreneurs offers the likeliest means of achieving these goals.

A scarcity of physicians in impoverished urban areas and in the world's geographically isolated rural areas makes delivery of even the most basic, preventive-medical care difficult if not impossible. But recent advances in two fields — remote diagnosis and home medical testing — are proving that quality health care and reasonable costs can go hand in hand.

Remote diagnosis, incorporating advances in computers and telecommunications, enables communities to avail themselves of state-of-the-art medical technological expertise well beyond the means of their local medical practitioner. In addition, when geographically remote or inner-city communities can avail themselves of these technologies only as necessary, they can focus resources on basic medical care provided by less costly medical professionals such as paramedics and nurse practitioners.

Like remote diagnosis, home health screening, medical testing, and diagnostic technology can save time, money, and lives. In addition, innovations in medication-delivery tools are enabling patients to self-administer oxygen, shots, and even intravenous food through a pump carried in a small nylon backpack. These products and services have been developed by medical entrepreneurs who saw better ways of meeting individual health care needs.

Environment. More than 30 years have passed since the first Earth Day, in April 1970, called the world's attention to the deteriorating state of the global environment. Since that first tolling bell of warning, we have become increasingly familiar with the chal-

169

lenges that confront us. Global warming and its greenhouse effect have continued unabated as waste gases, primarily carbon dioxide released by the combustion of oil, coal, and gas, continue to spew into the Earth's atmosphere. These same energy sources will one day be expended. Meanwhile, the world's waters and aquatic species are still being poisoned by acid rain, largely the result of sulfur dioxide released into the air by coal-burning power plants. The Earth-encircling ozone layer is less and less able to protect us from the life-threatening effects of the sun's ultraviolet rays as chlorofluorocarbons continue to eat away at this protective blanket. In tropical regions of the Third World, growing populations desperate for economic survival burn their forests to clear enough land to graze cattle or cultivate marketable crops, taking more and more tropical rain forests out of the increasingly precarious global ecological balance. The industrialized world's reliance on non-renewable resources guarantees the ongoing acceleration of these frightening trends.

Technology has enabled a multitude of innovative environmental solutions across a broad range of targets. Alternative, renewable energy sources such as solar photovoltaic cells, geothermal and solar-thermal generation, wind power, and hydrogen are no longer dismissed as fringe thinking. "Industrial ecology" became the manufacturing credo of the 1990s, as more and more companies understood that by redesigning manufacturing processes they could avoid using materials that end up as toxic waste and thereby avoid the costs associated with disposal or storage of toxic material.

Sustainable development is a goal we all must embrace. It is imperative to accept the fact that market-based environmentalism offers the most effective means of transferring technological advances into the areas of greatest need, ensuring that future generations inherit a land, not a landfill.

Public Television. The outstanding but beleaguered U.S. Public Broadcasting System (PBS) faces an array of circumstances that may cause it to change its vision and even create a new mission. PBS finds itself in an increasingly competitive environment because of the types of educational and cultural programming now available through cable television and direct broadcast systems.

In 1991, the Corporation for Public Broadcasting (CPB) commissioned an outside management study by the Boston Consulting Group, which recognized the changing TV broadcast environment and the necessity for programming changes and new funding strategies. The study laid out a strategic approach to making change.[3]

A separate, independent study and report released in 1993 by the Twentieth Century Fund was more comprehensive in its analysis and more complimentary in its praise of PBS's quality programming. This study also demanded change for PBS in recognition of the changes in the TV industry, the need for more and better purely educational programming, and the financial climate of the 1990s.[4]

Though almost all of PBS's programming is sometimes labeled as "educational," it is instructive to examine what resources are actually earmarked for certified TV educational courses. Total PBS revenue, from the CPB down to the local stations' fund-raising drives, was $1.5 billion[5] in 1994. From that total, $137 million was devoted to all educational programming, of which $8.2 million went to for-credit college telecourses. The $8.2 million represented one-half of one percent (0.5 percent)[6] of total public television expenditures, indicating that college credit telecourses were — and they still are — a relatively minor part of PBS programming (Figure 9).

Though public television serves many masters other than Instructional Television, consider the possibilities for instructional programming delivery if some of the annual CPB and PBS overhead budgets — close to $60 million in some years — could be redirected to acquire additional for-credit educational programming. As long as the CPB is governmentally funded, public debate is appropriate, and opportunities for Free Market Fusion exist within the PBS mission.

CHALLENGES ARE PLENTIFUL

The list of challenges we face is long and daunting. A quick hit list of social concerns might include the high dropout rate for high school minorities, illiteracy, child poverty, drug addiction, crime, AIDS, homelessness, overcrowded prisons and a sky-high recidivism rate, the need to increase the effectiveness and accessibility (financial as well as logistic) of our higher education resources, to re-incorporate seniors into productive societal roles, to mainstream the physically disabled back into society so that they can live inde-

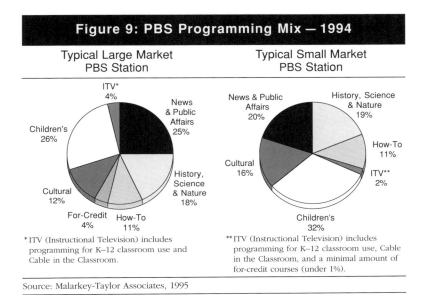

Figure 9: PBS Programming Mix — 1994

Typical Large Market
PBS Station

ITV* 4%
News & Public Affairs 25%
Children's 26%
History, Science & Nature 18%
Cultural 12%
For-Credit 4%
How-To 11%

* ITV (Instructional Television) includes programming for K–12 classroom use and Cable in the Classroom.

Typical Small Market
PBS Station

News & Public Affairs 20%
History, Science & Nature 19%
How-To 11%
ITV** 2%
Cultural 16%
Children's 32%

** ITV (Instructional Television) includes programming for K–12 classroom use, Cable in the Classroom, and a minimal amount of for-credit courses (under 1%).

Source: Malarkey-Taylor Associates, 1995

pendent lives and make the contributions they are capable of, and to provide adequate, affordable medical care.

The world is caught in a web of suffering that decades of goodwill, foreign aid, and well-intentioned but often fruitless efforts have failed to eradicate. The world hunger problem and its companion issues, overpopulation and poorly managed resources, seem by now incapable of solution. Yet are they?

Where do we begin? *How* do we begin? We can begin with Free Market Fusion.

THE LARGER ARENA: TAPPING ENTREPRENEURIAL TALENT

Why not go to the world's entrepreneurs and ask them for solutions? These are individuals trained to see the opportunities in change, the possibilities in dislocation. Not constrained by governmental structures or established processes, entrepreneurs are free to find the most effective ways to meet goals. Who knows what reordering of existing resources, what rethinking of current responses, we might achieve? We need to tap the creative energy and risk-taking spirit of those willing to operate in Buckminster Fuller's "outlaw area" of untried solutions and no guarantees.

I believe solutions are always possible. The key is to structure circumstances that nurture creative, innovative thinking so that our most innovative thinkers can design new solutions. It is obvious that when a society faces a problem that has continually resisted traditional means of resolution, other solutions must be invented and tried. It becomes necessary to think and create outside the structure of established assumptions and policies *with great speed.*

The challenges that have been described in this book and with which higher education must deal are formidable. What has become obvious is that the changes will occur. People who want higher education will find a way to get it and, with rapidly opening free markets, there will be suppliers.

The challenge to our world's higher education establishment is to accept this inevitable shift in its student market, to identify partners and technologies that will help it respond, and to set about, perhaps through Free Market Fusion, creating ways to be more effective educational suppliers in the 21st century.

---

[1]Thomas Jefferson, letter to Samuel Kercheval, 12 July 1816.

[2]Peter Drucker, *Innovation and Entrepreneurship: Principles and Practice* (New York: Harper & Row, 1985), 17.

[3]Corporation for Public Broadcasting, *Strategies for Public Television in a Multi-channel Environment: The Boston Consulting Group Study* (Washington, D.C.: March 1991).

[4]The Report of the Twentieth Century Fund Task Force on Public Television, *Quality Time?* (New York: The Twentieth Century Fund Press, 1993).

[5]Malarkey-Taylor Associates, *PBS Telecourse Study* (Washington, D.C.: May 1995).

[6]Malarkey-Taylor Associates, *Research Study on Public Broadcasting* (Washington, D.C.: March 1995).

**Tut, tut, child, said the Duchess.
Everything's got a moral if only you
can find it.**

> — Lewis Carroll,
> *Alice's Adventures in
> Wonderland*

Epilogue

The information revolution is ending. Long live the age of knowledge.

As some unnamed sage once quipped, "Successful revolutions hasten their own demise." This view couldn't more aptly describe what has happened to the much heralded information revolution, which has marked our world's transition from the industrial to the postindustrial era, or more appropriately, the knowledge age. The knowledge age will be an age of intelligent machines and convergent beings who gradually come to depend on computer chips and data banks to enhance their individual characters and capabilities. It will be revolutionary in impact and highly controversial. And technology will carry the day.

Second in importance to the changes brought about by a revolution are its artifacts, which represent the catalysts of change.

The valuable artifacts of the American Revolution are not its military paraphernalia but the colonial printing presses and the information they produced: Letters, newspapers, pamphlets, extracts of sermons and speeches, and, that singular document, the Declaration of Independence. Many of the documents predated the actual hostilities, or, in the case of the Declaration, clarified for posterity the passions that were unleashed after almost two decades of dissent and protest in the American colonies.

Never in the history of humankind had political discussion and debate been so effectively or spontaneously communicated as in the outpouring of political rhetoric flowing from the colonial presses. Thousands of cheap leaflets and pamphlets were printed, passed hand-to-hand, and reprinted so that the 13 colonies were literally papered with the ideas of democracy.

When future anthropologists sift through the artifacts of the information revolution, they will come across the skeletal outlines of electronic platforms, the communications organizations of the late 20th century that made our swift transition into the age of knowledge possible.

Electronic platforms are neurological in nature. In many ways they resemble the human brains they feed. They combine many concepts, pieces of circuitry, extensive delivery facilities, and content connected in neurological fashion. They are interconnected to act in concert, and, as more and more connectivity evolves, the platforms will become broader and deeper.

As electronic media, they look much like cable, telecommunications, and computer-based entities. They are transitory, morphing, enabling organizations that act as creators and purveyors of information, entertainment, and education. These evolving electronic platforms are changing, among other things, the nature of knowledge acquisition, especially teaching models as they have existed since the days of early Athens. Pedagogy has been turned on its ear.

At the moment of this writing, electronic platforms are transforming the globe's educational systems into cyberschools where knowledge is transformed into video and other electronic-media textbooks, lectures, demonstrations, and e-mail chat sessions among faculty and students. For those societies that are wealthy, the transition is coming almost overnight. For those that are poor, it is coming more slowly, but the wave of change is as inevitable as the wave of illiteracy eradication that has swept the world in the past 15 years. To be sure, the battle has not been won, but the new technologies of the Internet and various supporting telephony and satellite innovations will help propel it forward.

Electronic platforms not only guarantee delivery but also assure standards of excellence and act as a potent weapon against censorship and information control. They provide a level playing field, assuring that students who enter a cyberschool immediately have at their disposal vast resources of electronically stored and linked information resources that can quickly put them on a par with their contemporaries. These resources, combined with a willingness to manipulate them appropriately, also place the cyberstudent in the unique position of being able to question and challenge assumptions and hypotheses as never before.

The overlying contribution of cyberschools — and this includes such early innovators as the publicly funded Sunrise Semester and Star Schools, the private Jones International University and the growing number of open universities adopting electronic delivery — is that they transfer power to individuals. This power enables individuals to transform their own lives, regardless of whether they live in the rural reaches of the American West, the Australian out-back, or in the great, densely populated cities of South America and Asia.

Even though the economic wherewithal to access electronic platform technology is still an obstacle to the world's poor, this obstruction will be circumvented in a few short years by a new wave of cheap, universally accessible electronic platforms and net-works that will finally transform virtually every setting that has electric power — living rooms, one-room schoolhouses, and, yes, even one-room huts — into access points for the age of knowledge.

Education through electronic platforms has the added advan-tage of efficient delivery. Such delivery systems are free of much of the friction of traditional education and government bureaucra-cy that once kept education the exclusive domain and source of power for the elite. Quality assurance will remain an important part of institutional oversight, but accrediting organizations will change the way they view students and institutions.

Electronic platforms provided an augmentation to the world's educational systems in the late 20th century, but in the 21st centu-ry they will quickly emerge as the only economical solution to sat-isfy the increased global demand for education documented in the first chapter of this book. Importantly, they can provide "scale" of delivery and market access for educational solutions such as cyberschools. Still, no one existing institution, company, or industry can do it all; there is room for all to participate.

For educators who are reluctant to accept electronic educational delivery because of its unavoidable assault on cultural icons, I offer the assurance of philosophers from McLuhan to Plato. As McLuhan observed, TV — and we can extend this to electronic platforms of all kinds — created a new environment through which we observe the "old" environment of the industrial age, helping us understand and learn from it. Likewise, the industrial age transformed the Renaissance into an art form because of the new perspective through which it could be viewed. Plato, the scribe of Athens when writing was new, turned oral dialogue into art by documenting it.

It is my conviction that the technology and communications revolutions are propelling us into a new Renaissance, the knowledge age. This age will accelerate as the private side of our world economy and cultural life tackles the world's great problems and we begin to perceive these predicaments as opportunities, especially in education. The outcome can be a more peaceful world, a diverse vibrant world alive with new levels of expectation.

One of the evolving but ultimately predominant artifacts of the knowledge age will be cyberschools. Long live the age of knowledge.

Glenn R. Jones
August 2000

APPENDIX A — Principles for Distance Learning

THE WESTERN INTERSTATE COMMISSION FOR HIGHER EDUCATION'S (WICHE) PRINCIPLES OF GOOD PRACTICE FOR ELECTRONICALLY OFFERED ACADEMIC DEGREE AND CERTIFICATE PROGRAMS

The following is the complete text of the WICHE principles.

Preamble

These principles are the product of a Western Cooperative for Educational Telecommunications project, "Balancing Quality and Access: Reducing State Policy Barriers to Electronically Delivered Higher Education Programs."

The three-year project, supported by the U.S. Department of Education's Fund for the Improvement of Postsecondary Education, is designed to foster an interstate environment that encourages the electronic provision of quality higher education programs across state lines. The principles have been developed by a group representing the Western states higher education regulating agencies, higher education institutions, and the regional accrediting community.

Recognizing that the context for learning in our society is undergoing profound changes, those charged with developing the principles have tried not to tie them to or compare them to, traditional campus structures. The principles are also designed to be sufficiently flexible that institutions offering a range of programs — from graduate degree to certificates — will find them useful.

Several assumptions form the basis for these principles:

- The electronically offered program is provided by or through an institution that is accredited by a nationally recognized accrediting body.

- The institution's programs holding specialized accreditation meet the same requirements when offered electronically.

- The institution may be a traditional higher education institution, a consortium of such institutions, or another type of organization or entity.

- The principles address programs rather than individual courses.

- It is the institution's responsibility to review educational programs it provides via technology in terms of its own internal definitions of these principles.

PRINCIPLES

Curriculum and Instruction

1. Each electronically offered program of study results in learning outcomes appropriate to the rigor and breadth of the degree or certificate awarded.

2. An electronically offered degree or certificate program is coherent and complete.

3. The program provides for appropriate real-time or delayed interaction between faculty and students and among students.

4. Qualified faculty provide appropriate oversight of the program electronically offered.

Institutional Context and Commitment to Role and Mission

5. The program is consistent with the institution's role and mission.

6. Review and approval processes ensure the appropriateness of the technology being used to meet the program's objectives.

Faculty Support

7. The program provides faculty support services specifically related to teaching via an electronic system.

8. The program provides training for faculty who teach via the use of technology.

Resources for Learning

9. The program ensures appropriate learning resources are available to students.

Students and Student Services

10. The program provides students with clear, complete, and timely information on the curriculum, course and degree requirements, nature of faculty/student interaction, assumptions about technological competence and skills, technical equipment requirements, availability of academic support services and financial aid resources, and costs and payment policies.

11. The enrolled students have reasonable and adequate access to the range of student services appropriate to support their learning. That accepted students have the background, knowledge, and technical skills needed to undertake the program.

12. Advertising, recruiting, and admissions materials clearly and accurately represent the program and the services available.

Commitment to Support

13. Policies for faculty evaluation include appropriate consideration of teaching and scholarly activities related to electronically offered programs.

14. The institution demonstrates a commitment to ongoing support, both financial and technical, and to continuation of the program for a period sufficient to enable students to complete a degree/certificate.

Evaluation and Assessment

15. The institution evaluates the program's educational effectiveness, including assessments of student learning outcomes, student retention, and student and faculty satisfaction.

16. Students have access to such program evaluation data.

17. The institution provides for assessment and documentation of student achievement in each course and at completion of the program.[1]

THE AMERICAN COUNCIL ON EDUCATION, CENTER FOR ADULT LEARNING AND EDUCATIONAL CREDENTIALS' GUIDING PRINCIPLES FOR DISTANCE LEARNING IN A LEARNING SOCIETY

The following is the complete text of the American Council on Education's Guiding Principles for Distance Learning, including a statement of the principles' core values. (Draft released May 1996.)

CORE VALUES

These principles assume that the practice of distance learning contributes to the larger social mission of education and training in a democratic society. With that in mind, the principles reflect the following tenets and values:

- Learning is a lifelong process, important to successful participation in the social, cultural, civic, and economic life of a democratic society.

- Lifelong learning involves the development of a range of learning skills and behaviors that should be explicit outcomes of learning activities.

- The diversity of learners, learning needs, learning context, and modes of learning must be recognized if the learning activities are to achieve their goals.

- All members of society have the right to access learning opportunities that provide the means for effective participation in society.

- Participation in a learning society involves both rights and responsibilities for learners, providers, and those charged with the oversight of learning.

- Because learning is social and sensitive to context, learning experiences should support interaction and the development of learning communities, whether social, public, or professional.

- The development of a learning society may require significant changes in the roles, responsibilities, and activities of provider organizations and personnel as well as of the learners themselves.

PRINCIPLES

1. Distance learning activities are designed to fit the specific context for learning.

   a) Learning opportunities include a clear statement of intended learning outcomes, learning content that is appropriate to those outcomes, clear expectations of learner activities, flexible opportunities for interactions, and assessment methods appropriate to the activities and technologies.

   b) Elements of a learning event — the learning content, instructional methods, technologies, and context — complement each other.

   c) The selection and application of technologies for a specific learning opportunity are appropriate for the intended learning outcomes, subject matter content, relevant charac-teristics and circumstances of the learner, and cost range.

d) Learning activities and modes of assessment are responsible to the learning needs of individual learners.

e) The learning experience is organized to increase learner control over the time, place, and pace of instruction.

f) Learning outcomes address both content mastery and increased learning skills.

g) Individuals with specialized skills in content, instructional methods, or technologies work collaboratively as a design team to create learning opportunities.

h) The learning design is evaluated on a regular basis for effec-tiveness, with findings utilized as a basis for improvement.

2. Distance learning opportunities are effectively supported for learners through fully accessible modes of delivery and resources.

a) The providing organization has a learner support system to assist the learner in effectively using the resources provid-ed. This system includes technology and technical support, site facilitation, library and information services, advising, counseling, and problem-solving assistance.

b) The provider considers the needs for learner support in relation to the distance learning mode(s) used and makes provision for delivery of appropriate resources based on the design of the learning activities, the technology involved, and the needs of the learner.

c) Access to support services — such as scheduling, registration, and record keeping — is convenient, efficient, and responsive to diverse learners as well as consistent with other elements of the delivery system.

d) Support systems are accessible to and usable by the learners and are sufficiently flexible to accommodate different learning styles.

e) The provider discloses to the learner all information pertinent to the learning opportunity — such as course prerequisites, modes of study, evaluation criteria, and technical needs — and provides some form of orientation for those desiring it.

f) Support systems for learning opportunity are reviewed regularly to ensure their currency and effectiveness.

3. Distance learning initiatives must be backed by an organizational commitment to quality and effectiveness in all aspects of the learning environment.

a) Involvement in distance learning is consistent with the overall mission of the provider; policies regarding distance learning are integrated into the provider's overall policy framework.

b) The providing organization makes a financial and administrative commitment to maintain distance learning programs through completion and to support faculty and learner services needed to ensure an effective learning environment.

c) Administrative and support systems (registration, advising, assessment, etc.) are compatible with the learning delivery system to ensure a coherent learning environment.

d) The organization's curricular and administrative policies incorporate the needs of distance learning as well as traditional learning activities.

e) The provider makes a commitment to research and development of distance learning, maintaining a systematic evaluation of the content, processes, and support systems involved in its distance learning activities.

f) The provider makes a concomitant investment of resources and effort in professional development and support of both faculty and staff involved in distance learning.

g) The providing organization recognizes effective participation in distance learning in its promotion and reward system for faculty and staff and ensures that its policies regarding promotion, tenure (if applicable), and departmental/program funding reflect the integration of distance learning into the organization's mission.

h) The policies, management practices, learning design process, and operational procedures for distance learning are regularly evaluated to ensure effectiveness and currency.

i) The provider does not distinguish between learning accomplished at a distance and learning accomplished through other means in recognizing learner achievement.

4. Distance education programs organize learning activities around demonstrable learning outcomes, assist the learner to achieve these outcomes, and assess learner progress by reference to these outcomes.

a) When possible, individual learners help shape the learning outcomes and how they are achieved.

b) Intended learning outcomes are described in observable, measurable, and achievable terms.

c) The learning design is consistent with and shaped to achieve the intended learning outcomes.

d) Distance education media and delivery systems are used in a way that facilitates the achievement of intended learning outcomes.

e) Learning outcomes are assessed in a way relevant to the content, the learner's situation, and the distance education delivery system.

f) Assessment of learning is timely, appropriate, and responsive to the needs of the learner.

g) Intended learning outcomes are reviewed regularly to assure their clarity, utility, and appropriateness for the learners.

5. The provider has a plan and infrastructure for using technology that support its learning goals and activities.

a) The technology plan defines the technical requirement and compatibility needed to support the learning activity.

b) The technology plan addresses system security to assure the integrity and validity of information shared in the learning activities.

c) The technology facilitates interactivity among all elements of a learning environment and places a high value on ease of use by learners.

d) The technology selected for distance learning is fully accessible and understandable to learners and has the power necessary to support its intended use.

e) Providers communicate the purpose of the technologies used for learning and, through training, assist learners, faculty, and staff to understand its etiquette, acquire the knowledge and skills to manipulate and interact with it, and understand the objectives and outcomes that the technologies are intended to support.

f) The technology infrastructure meets the needs of both learners and learning facilitators for presenting information, interacting within the learning community, and gaining access to learning resources.[2]

---

[1]Sally M. Johnstone and B. Krauth, "Some Principles of Good Practice for the Virtual University," *Change*, March–April 1996, 40.

[2]Eugene Sullivan and T. Rocco, co-chairs, Task Force on Distance Learning, "Guiding Principles for Distance Learning in a Learning Society," draft copy (May 1996), 3–5.

Global Alliance for Transnational Education (GATE)

Definitions

For some years, people have used the term "global village" to denote the great ease and speed with which we can now interact with people in distant locations. Increasingly, this effect is being felt in education also. Whatever the reasons — whether cultural or academic, economic, or political — educational activities are becoming even more mobile, and this mobility does not stop at national boundaries (Woodhouse & Craft, 1993). Mobile education has a different set of characteristics from place-bound education, and transnational education brings yet more features. To ground the issues and processes discussed in GATE's certification manual, the following definition is used:

Transnational education (TNE) denotes any teaching or learning activity in which the students are in a different country (the host country) from that in which the institution providing the education is based (the home country). This situation requires that national boundaries be crossed by information related to the education and by staff or educational materials (whether the information and the materials travel by mail, computer network, radio or television broadcast, or other means).

Examples of Transnational Education (TNE)

As is implied by the definition of TNE, it has many forms and variants. The following examples are therefore not exhaustive but intended to give a flavor of some possibilities:

On-line and distance education programs: distance education programs that are delivered — through Internet, Web, satellites, computers, correspondence, or other technological means — across national boundaries.

Branch campus: a campus set up by an institution in one country to provide its educational programs to students in another country.

Franchise: an institution (A) approves an institution (B) in another country to provide one or more of institution A's programs to students in institution B's country.

Articulation: the systematic recognition by an institution (A) of specified study at an institution (B) in another country as partial credit towards a program at institution A.

Twinning: agreements between institutions in different countries to offer joint programs.

Corporate programs: programs offered by large corporations for academic credit from institutions; this often involves crediting across national borders. Some countries, notably the United States, have set up foreign programs for their own citizens or students but have then opened the programs to other students (see for example Deupree & Lenn, 1997). These include study-abroad programs initiated for U.S. students of U.S. institutions, and programs established for the American expatriate community. Almost 400 U.S. higher education institutions provide credit-generating programs leading to degrees at almost 200 U.S. military bases around the world, and these programs are now generally open to citizens of the country in which the base is located.

Just like educational programs located within one country, transnational programs vary enormously in scope. Some are very general, whereas others are precisely targeted in some way, concentrating on a specific profession or need, such as an MBA, a graduate program in engineering, or a program for English as a Second Language.

GATE's primary purpose is to assure and improve the quality of education that crosses national borders.

THE CODE OF PRACTICE

GATE has drawn up a set of Principles for Transnational Education. There is wide agreement that any higher education institution providing education that crosses national boundaries should adhere to such principles as a matter of integrity and responsibility and to ensure the quality of the educational services. In addition, some governments and some corporations are expressing interest in having institutions adhere to such principles as a guarantee of quality and comparability of qualifications.

PRINCIPLES FOR TRANSNATIONAL EDUCATION

OVERVIEW

1. Goals and Objectives. Transnational courses must be guided by goals and objectives understood by participants who enroll in them and must fit appropriately within the provider's mission and expertise.

2. Standards. Students receiving education and educational credentials through transnational courses must be assured by the provider that these courses have been approved by the provider and meet its criteria for educational quality and that the same standards are applied, regardless of the place or manner in which the courses are provided.

3. Legal and Ethical Matters. Transnational courses must comply with all appropriate laws and requirements of the host country.

4. Student Enrollment and Admission. Participants in transnational courses must be treated equitably and ethically. In particular, all pertinent information must be disclosed to the participants, and each participant must hold full student status or its equivalent with the provider organization.

5. Human Resources. The provider organization must have a sufficient number of fully qualified people engaged in providing the transnational courses, and their activities must be supervised and regularly evaluated as a normal activity of the provider.

6. Physical and Financial Resources. The provider organization must ensure an adequate learning environment and sufficient resources for the transnational courses, and must provide assurance that adequate resources will continue to be available until all obligations to enrolled participants are fulfilled.

7. Teaching and Learning. Transnational courses must be pedagogically sound with respect to the methods of teaching and the nature and needs of the participants.

8. Student Support. The provider organization must provide students with adequate support services to maximize the potential benefit they receive from the transnational courses.

9. Evaluation. Transnational courses must be regularly and appropriately evaluated as a normal part of the provider organization's activities, with the results of the evaluations being used to improve these courses.

10. Third Parties. When third parties, such as agents or collaborating institutions, are involved in the TNE, there must be explicit written agreements covering their roles, expectations, and obligations.

CERTIFICATION

FOCUS

GATE is able to review an institution to ascertain whether:

- it has the appropriate systems in place to enable it to adhere to the Principles,

- it is in fact adhering to them in its actions,

- it has procedures for remedying the situation should faults occur, and

- the TNE provided is of a good standard.

A positive outcome to the review results in GATE certification of the institution.

RATIONALE

An institution may find GATE certification valuable for any or several of the following reasons:

- to demonstrate commitment to quality education

- certification is required by a country to permit a foreign institution to offer a program

- certification is accepted by a country for the purpose of recognizing the institution's graduates

- to ensure or enhance the employability of graduates

- to provide international comparability

- to facilitate international mobility

- to permit transportability of qualifications and partial qualifications

- to permit accumulation of international credits

- to gain exemption from other forms of accreditation

- to attract students

A government or rational system may find GATE certification valuable for some of the same reasons. In addition, governments and national systems may wish to use GATE certification as a check on the quality of education being exported by or imported into the country. Another systemic use of GATE certification would be to assist in an international credit bank situation, in which there is a need for a central repository and a central system of quality assurance.

The focus of GATE certification is consumer protection. It is intended not only to assess the existence and effectiveness of the procedures currently in place for achieving quality but also to facilitate their improvement. Therefore, although certification is a yes/no decision, GATE normally provides recommendations for improvement in either case. GATE may also comment on the type of institution or the designation of its programs.

OUTLINE OF THE CERTIFICATION PROCESS

OVERVIEW

GATE uses the standard international process of appointing a panel to consider a self-review report produced by the institution, to visit the institution, and to report to the GATE board, which then makes the final decision on certification. The extent of panel visitation undertaken depends on the circumstances of the particular institution and its activities but normally involves some or all of the panel visiting the home base or campus of the institution and at least one location abroad.

INITIATING THE CERTIFICATION PROCESS

Originator

The users of certification can be grouped into two categories — the providers or exporters of TNE and the receivers or importers of TNE. In either category, there may be institutions, national systems, and governments GATE review for certification may be requested by an institution or by the government or an EQA (External Quality Assurance) body in either the provider country (the home country) or a receiving country (a host country).

The request might originate in the home country if that country has no EQA system or if its EQA system does not check the transnational operations of its institutions, but the country (or its institutions) is concerned about their standing in other countries. The country might prefer to engage GATE to carry out this certification process rather than building internal expertise and procedures for the task, especially if only a few institutions are involved. An extension of this situation is when a country has no EQA system, but the country (or an institution within it) wants a global stamp of approval for the institution's quality. In this case, GATE would need to extend its review process beyond the transnational operations of the institution(s).

The request might originate in the host country if the country requires that transnational programs be certified before it will allow its citizens to enroll in them or will recognize the qualifications awarded. The host country may not have a checking mechanism of its own; and even if it has, it may prefer the transnational educational activities of provider institutions to be checked by an independent international body.

The request may originate from an institution, in any country, whether it is under the aegis of an EQA system or not, if the institution wishes to go through an international quality assurance process for its transnational activities or more generally.

Regardless of the origin of the request, review of an institution by GATE requires that institution's agreement and cooperation. Therefore, on receiving such a request from a source other than an institution, one of GATE's first acts is to contact the institution. Thereafter, the certification process is likely to be nearly the same as if the initial contact had been made by the institution. Except where otherwise stated, the certification manual is written as if the request originated with the institution. Variants required for the other cases are mentioned, as appropriate.

Scope

In requesting GATE certification, an institution specifies the desired scope of certification, e.g., which programs, which locations, or which types of program (such as undergraduate or continuing education). An outline of the information required from an institution requesting GATE certification, along with information on costs, can be found in Appendix C of the full certification manual (contact the GATE office to receive a copy). When GATE receives an application for certification, the certification coordinator contacts the institution to ensure that GATE understands the institution's structure and operations with respect to TNE and the extent and scope of the certification sought. With this information it should be possible to determine the likely nature and destination of visits by the review panel. Clarification may require a visit to the institution's home campus but is normally carried out by correspondence. If a visit is necessary, it would normally be made by the certification coordinator, but may be made by an experienced GATE reviewer who is geographically closer to the campus.

Extension of Scope

The certification process requires checking institutional and program structures. A later request for certification of other programs, during the period in which an earlier certification is still valid, would not require the institutional aspects to be rechecked.

Appointment of Review Panel

Once GATE has a firm certification request, the chair of the GATE Academic Advisory Committee selects potential members for a review panel. The selection is made from a committee-approved register of reviewers and takes into account any special characteristics of the institution, the need to have a panel that is coherent and balanced in background and experience, and the need to avoid conflicts of interest. Panels usually comprise three members, one of whom is a member of the GATE Academic Advisory Committee. If there is one predominant country in which the educational program is being provided or one such country that has specifically requested a review, it may be appropriate to have a panel member from that country as well. In addition, the institution may nominate a member to the panel.

When a small group of potential panel members has been identified, the institution is invited, in confidence, to indicate whether it is aware of any reason why any of those panelists should not be involved in auditing the university. Valid reasons could involve known or probable conflicts of interest or inappropriateness for the character of the institution. This does not give the institution a veto on panel membership: GATE must be convinced of the validity of the concern. Once panel membership has been finalized, one member (normally not the GATE Academic Advisory Committee member or the institutional nominee) is appointed by GATE as panel chair.

GATE is willing to consider proposals for simplifying or streamlining the certification process in particular cases, provided the rigor and integrity of the process is maintained. For example, it may be possible for a GATE nominee to be included in appropriate stages of an existing quality assurance process, whether at the national or institutional level. GATE would require adequate advance notice of such a proposal.

Institutional Self-Study

In order to obtain GATE certification, it is not sufficient for an institution simply to provide a description of its operating procedures for verification that they conform to the principles for TNE. Certification is about students' actual experiences, not merely what the written procedures promise. The GATE review panel therefore requires evidence of what actually occurs, and in order to provide this evidence, the institution itself must first collect it. This suggests the value of a critical institutional self-study preceding the certification process. The review panel can then perform a verification and reporting role. GATE is interested not only in checking systems but also in enhancing them, and an institutional self-study assists in this aim. A self-study usually reveals to an institution shortcomings and possibilities for improvement, and the institutional commitment required for the self-study prompts the institution to act on its findings.

In the self-study, the institution will ask itself questions implied or suggested by the principles for TNE: What are the procedures? Are they appropriate? Are they effective? How do we know? The starting point for the self-study, and for the review panel's investigation later, is the institution's own intentions with respect to its transnational educational activities. This self-study results in the presentation to GATE of a written dossier that outlines the systems relating to the institution's provision of TNE and the institution's assessment of the effectiveness of these systems.

The institution decides how long it intends to spend on the self-study and plans accordingly. It may begin the self-study process after it approaches GATE or long before. The self-study may be carried out specifically for GATE certification, for some other external review, or as part of the institution's internal quality assurance procedures.

Panel Consideration of Self-Study Dossier

When the dossier is sent to the chair of the GATE Academic Advisory Committee, it is distributed to members of the review panel. The reviewers examine the dossier to determine the nature and effectiveness of the system described, and how much detailed checking is required. The reviewers then share their first impressions of the portfolio and identify any further information or clarification required from the institution. This panel interaction may be via e-mail discussion or teleconferencing. The panel selects specific topics for investigation, decides on approaches to adopt, and considers what visits will be necessary. The panel's activities are likely to include sampling and detailed investigation of some programs, locations, and processes. All communication between the institution and members of the panel is via the panel chair (copies are sent to the chair of the GATE Academic Advisory Committee).

About three months is allowed between submission of the dossier and panel visits to the institution, during which time the panel chair and the institution map out a visit program. This normally requires further clarification of structural issues and the responsibilities of various committees. The visit program should be finalized no less than four weeks before the date of the first panel visit.

Visit to Home Campus

The program of visits drawn up by a review panel varies greatly, depending on the institution's structure and operations with regard to TNE and on the certification requested. In all cases, a visit is made to the institution's home campus to ensure that appropriate institutional procedures are in place. This visit usually involves the whole panel. If relevant programs are being offered at the institution's home campus, they will be inspected.

Throughout the certification process, the GATE board and the review panel consider modes of communication that permit participation at a distance, or by a subset of the panel, to reduce the traveling involved. If GATE were included in the national or institutional quality assurance process, home campus activities might be able to be covered at that stage, allowing the review panel to omit this step.

Visit to Sample Programs

To ensure that the institution's procedures are working as they should, the panel needs to see some instances of them in operation. If certification is being sought for a single program offered at one foreign location, that location is visited. If the certification is for one program offered at a number of locations, a sampling of the locations is visited. The institution provides full information on all locations, and the sample locations are selected by the panel. The same approach is taken if an institution is seeking institutional certification for all its TNE activities, but a wider sample is likely to be necessary.

In all cases, the number of foreign sites that need to be visited depends on the extent to which the quality assurance processes are centrally organized and monitored. For example, if three departments independently offer three programs, all three need to be inspected, but if the three departmental offerings are co-coordinated by a central institutional "international education office," visiting only one of them may be adequate.

During its visits, the panel meets a range of staff and students, normally including the head of the institution, members of relevant committees, and staff involved with sample programs.

Review Report

Following the visits, a report is produced describing the panel's findings in relation to the issues it has considered and its recommendations with respect to certification. A draft report is sent to the institution for comment on facts and emphasis. When finalized, the report is sent to the GATE Academic Advisory Committee.

The Decision

Based on the recommendations of the review panel, the GATE Academic Advisory Committee decides whether the institution should be certified. In either case, the decision is usually accompanied by suggestions from the panel for improvement and in the latter case, by reasons for the failure.

The yes/no decision is public, but the report is confidential to the panel, the Academic Advisory Committee, and the institution. If certification is granted, the certification period is normally for five years. If the certification process is unsuccessful, GATE can discuss with the institution whether the shortcomings appear to be addressable fairly quickly and whether in this case conducting a further review would be possible only a short time later.

Following the review, and as part of its own quality assurance procedures, GATE invites the institution and the review panel members to comment on the review process.

Typical Time Scale

GATE requires at least three months' notice before submission of the institution's self-study dossier and aims to carry out the first visit within three months of receiving the dossier. The goal is to make a decision within one year of receiving an application.

Appendix C — Key Internet Addresses

Address	Institution
www.ACENET.edu	American Council on Education
www.open.ac.uk	British Open University
www.uwex.edu/disted/home.html	Distance Education Clearing House
www.fielding.edu	The Fielding Institute
www.edugate.org	Global Alliance for Transnational Education (GATE)
www.gsn.org	The Global Schoolhouse
www.e-education.com	Jones education software
www.JonesKnowledge.com	Jones education software and services
www.jones.com/egl.html	Jones's e-global Library
www.jones.com	Jones International, Ltd., Corporate Web Portal
www.jonesinternational.edu	Jones International University
www.McLuhan.utoronto.ca/site/content_marshall.html	Marshall McLuhan
www.mty.itesm.mx	Monterrey Institute of Technology
http://rs6.loc.gov/amhome.html	National Digital Library (U.S. Library of Congress)
www.ntu.edu	National Technological University
www.oclc.org/oclc	On-Line Computer Library Center
www.tui.edu	The Union Institute
www.phoenix.edu	University of Phoenix
www.wiche.edu	Western Interstate Commission for Higher Education